How to Know People by their Hands

by Josef Ranald

WITH ILLUSTRATIONS

British Library Cataloguing-in-Publication Data
A catalogue record for this book is available from the
British Library

Palmistry

Palmistry, or 'chiromancy' (from the Greek *kheir* meaning 'hand' and *manteia* meaning 'divination'), is the claim of characterization and foretelling the future through the study of the palm. The practice is found all over the world, with numerous cultural variations, and those who practice chiromancy are generally called palmists, palm readers, hand readers, hand analysts, or chirologists.

Palmistry generally consists of the practice of evaluating a person's character or future life by 'reading' the palm of that person's hand. Various 'lines' (heart line, life line, etc.) and 'mounts' (or bumps), purportedly suggest interpretations by their relative sizes, qualities, and intersections. In some traditions, readers also examine characteristics of the fingers, fingernails, fingerprints, and palmar skin patterns (dermatoglyphics), skin texture and colour, shape of the palm, and flexibility of the hand. A reader usually begins by looking at the person's 'dominant hand' (the hand he or she writes with or uses the most, which is sometimes considered to represent the conscious mind, whereas the other hand is subconscious). In some traditions of palmistry, the other hand is believed to carry hereditary or family traits, or, depending on the palmist's cosmological beliefs, to convey information about past-life or karmic conditions.

Though there are debates on which hand is better to read from, both have their own significance. It is customary to assume that the left hand shows potential in an individual, and the right shows realized personality. The basic framework for 'Classical' palmistry (the most widely taught and practiced tradition) is rooted in Greek mythology. Each area of the palm and fingers is related to a god or goddess, and the features of that area indicate the nature of the corresponding aspect of the subject. For example, the ring finger is associated with the Greek god Apollo; characteristics of the ring finger are tied to the subject's dealings with art, music, aesthetics, fame, wealth, and harmony.

There are three main lines on almost all hands, generally given the most weight by palmists: 'the heart line' (representing love and attraction), 'the head line' (representing the person's mind and the way it works, i.e. learning, intellectualism and communication), and 'the life line' – perhaps the most controversial line on the hand, believed to represent the person's vitality and vigour, physical health and general well being. The life line is also believed to reflect major life changes, including cataclysmic events, physical injuries, and relocations. Contrary to popular belief, modern palmists generally do not believe that the length of a person's life line is tied to the length of a person's existence.

Palmistry has a long history, and is a practice common to many different places on the Eurasian landmass; it has been practised in the cultures of India, Tibet, China, Persia, Sumeria, Ancient Israel and Babylonia. According to some, it had its roots in Hindu Astrology (known in Sanskrit as 'Jyotish'), Chinese Yijing ('I Ching'), and Roma fortune tellers. Several thousand years ago, the Hindu sage Valmiki is thought to have written a book comprising 567 stanzas, the title of which translates in English as *The Teachings of Valmiki Maharshi on Male Palmistry*. From India, the art of palmistry spread to China, Tibet, Egypt, Persia and to other countries in Europe.

From China, palmistry progressed to Greece where Anaxagoras practiced it. Aristotle (384 - 322 BCE) discovered a treatise on the subject of palmistry on an altar of Hermes, which he then presented to Alexander the Great, who took great interest in examining the character of his officers by analyzing the lines on their hands. Aristotle stated that 'Lines are not written into the human hand without reason. They emanate from heavenly influences and man's own individuality.' Accordingly, Aristotle, Hippocrates and Alexander the Great popularized the laws and practice of palmistry. Hippocrates even sought to use palmistry to aid his clinical procedures.

During the Middle Ages the art of palmistry was actively suppressed by the Catholic Church as pagan superstition. In Renaissance magic, palmistry was classified as one of the seven 'forbidden arts', along with necromancy, geomancy, aeromancy, pyromancy, hydromancy, and spatulamancy. It experienced a revival in the modern era however, starting with Captain Casimir Stanislas D'Arpentigny and his publication of *La Chirognomie* in 1839. The 'Chirological Society of Great Britain' was founded in London by Katherine St Hill in 1889 with the stated aim of 'advancing and systematising the art of palmistry and to prevent charlatans from abusing the art.' Edgar de Valcourt-Vermont (Comte de St Germain) founded the 'American Chirological Society' in 1897.

A pivotal figure in the modern palmistry movement was the Irish William John Warner, known by his sobriquet, 'Cheiro'. After studying under gurus in India he set up a palmistry practice in London and enjoyed a wide following of famous clients from around the world, including famous celebrities like Mark Twain, W. T. Stead, Sarah Bernhardt, Mata Hari, Oscar Wilde, Thomas Edison, the Prince of Wales, General Kitchener, William Ewart Gladstone, and Joseph Chamberlain. So popular was Cheiro as a 'Society Palmist' that even those who were not believers in the occult had their hands read by him. The skeptical Mark Twain wrote in Cheiro's visitor's book that he had '...exposed my character to me with humiliating accuracy.'

Criticism of palmistry often rests with the lack of empirical evidence supporting its efficacy. Scientific literature typically regards palmistry as a pseudoscientific or superstitious belief, and skeptics often include palmists on lists of alleged psychics who practice cold reading. Despite this skepticism, palmistry is a practice and branch of human endeavour with an intriguing history – and whether it has any truth or not, provides a fascinating window into folkloric and religious beliefs more generally. We hope the reader enjoys this book on the subject.

TABLE OF CONTENTS

CONTENTS *Continued*

PART II. THE DOCTOR LOOKS AT HANDS

PART III. THE HAND AS MEDIUM FOR IDENTIFICATION

PART IV. THE HAND AS VOCATIONAL GUIDE

PART V. ANALYSES OF SOME FAMOUS HANDS

CONTENTS *Continued*

PART VI

PART VII

SENSITIZED SHEETS

INTRODUCTION

SOME time ago there was an eclipse of the sun. To study this phenomenon, scientific expeditions began to gather their equipment many months in advance. They knew what instruments would be needed, where to go for their observations, and the exact moment when the event would take place. This eclipse was foreseen even before the birth of the scientists taking part in the expeditions.

Was this a case of clairvoyance—penetration of the future by some gifted seer whose word was accepted by modern scientists as sufficient reason to send them voyaging thousands of miles? Not at all. Test tubes and mathematical formulæ breed men from Missouri who want to be shown. They would certainly not have accepted the word of inspiration on this subject any more than they would have taken a mad Adventist's forecast of the world's end. Yet they, and millions of others, accepted detailed predictions of the exact path the obscuring shadow of the moon would take.

So, in other fields of science, has prediction become a matter of course. Chemists will tell you in advance the reaction to be obtained by combining two substances. Physicists will explain how soon and where a projectile, shot from a certain place, will hit. Engineers will inform you how many revolutions per minute to expect from a wheel as the power applied is increased or decreased.

In less learned circles, everyone is willing to embark on limited predictions about the everyday occurrences of our lives. We take for granted that night will be followed by morning. We assume that when we apply a match to an open gas jet the gas will ignite. We are not surprised when we drop a pencil to see it fall to the ground.

Quite clearly, we translate a repeated occurrence into prediction of its continuance. The scientist does not go that far. His predictions are based on involved calculations making use of past observations. In theory he is not so certain even as you that the sun will rise tomorrow, for his mathematical formulæ express only the probability of such an event, not its certainty. Theoretically, his statistics give him nothing but the betting odds for and against. In practice, however, he is able to figure the exact shift from yesterday's path, both in time and position, by which tomorrow's sunrise will differ from yesterday's.

What I am trying to say is that the scientist, though he lays no claims to an ability to make certain predictions, actually does make predictions daily and has them accepted as valid both by his colleagues and by the general public.

Strangely enough, the one subject which scientists have not brought into conformity with their formulæ of statistical averages is man himself. By and large man is completely unpredictable to himself. Man's own activities, his reactions, his thoughts, the various complex factors which make up the individual are today probably less understood than any other natural phenomenon.

The results of this course are evident everywhere. This era is characterized by a general breakdown. In Europe a whole generation lives from hand to mouth, making no plans for the future, dreading a war which seems to it inevitable. The thought of chaos and death is part of every European youth. In Asia the dam has already burst, and men are senselessly murdering each other.

Statesmanship has proved itself a self-seeking Frankenstein. Perhaps it is now time for scientists to take the helm instead of statesmen and generals. Man has lost his fear of thunderstorms as he has come to understand them. What he most fears now is his fellows. I believe that with complete understanding of himself that fear too would disappear. ˙

It seems to me that science should revolt from its subservience to cruelty and greed and put itself at the service of the human race. Its service would have to stem from complete understanding. Picture to yourself a great brotherhood of men of science intent on studying man for his own salvation. Finding the scientific leaders of this day—Carrel, Jeans, Eddington, Einstein, Huxley, Russell—concerned about the human race gives promise that such a brotherhood may some time be realized. In that promise, I believe, lies eventual freedom for the majority of men from subjection to their fellows.

Of course, we have had students of man in the past, but to date they have divided their subject into at least two separate parts. The first part, which took in the physical aspect of man, has made considerable headway, though, compared with the degree of certainty which governs other scientific studies, this too is still in its infancy. The second division, man's study of his mentality, personality, consciousness, psyche—you can call it what you will—is very far behind.

One reason for the lag, it seems to me, is that the division into physical and mental compartments is an artificial one. Man is a whole who acts and reacts as a whole. There is no physician who will deny the interrelation between his patient's spirits and his recovery from a dangerous illness. There is no psychologist who will not admit the effect of a disease on the behavior of his subject. Why then let names like psychology, physiology, biology prevent us from considering man as an entity?

Instead of regarding the "mental" and "physical" as two distinct things, many modern scientists are uniting them. The leaders of scientific thought see both aspects of man as parts of one integrated whole, the study of which some have called "psychobiology," a combined science of man's mental and physical being. To this new science they are bringing the methods of objective measurement which they use in the laboratory. If plotting statistical probabilities has become the foundation of chemistry and physics, that coldly impersonal method can also be used in dealing with the science of human beings.

There is still another thing we can learn from the exact sciences. In their conclusions, scientists make use of all the evidence presented. In studying human beings, many of our theorists have built schools of thought around isolated sets of phenomena. Behaviorists denied that anything but physical actions and reactions could be studied. Freud placed us all in a half-world governed by repressed sex instincts. Others claim that diet alone makes the man. Why not look at all the evidence?

It was with some such idea that I began to write this book about hand analysis. In a comprehensive study of man, the study of his hands will, I am certain, play a part.

It is unfortunate that this subject has for so long been associated with charlatanry and fortune telling. Most of us think of crystal gazing and reading hands as very much the same thing. I myself began my study of hands in a spirit of skepticism. In the first place, palmistry, as I then thought of it, was associated with the death of my best friend, a young fellow-officer in the Austrian army. Consequently, I not only doubted that there was anything to handreading, but I very much resented its pretensions.

My friend and I were on leave from front line warfare in 1917. As a lark, he proposed taking me to a university professor who read hands as a hobby. I laughed at the idea, but we went.

Almost the first words of this student of hands were that he saw fear of death indicated in my friend's hand—more than that, as the indication was repeated in both hands, the old man predicted the early death of my friend.

I became angry. "A safe prediction for you old men sitting at home," I told him. "What one of us in the trenches does not fear death? And for how many of us can you not foretell the end within a very short time? Tell me, have I also a week?"

The old man looked at my hand. "No," he said. "You will live a long time. You will have many narrow escapes, it is true, many adventures. You will meet the great men of this age, travel all over the world."

Going back on duty I was still bitter about the professor's remark to my friend. Of course, there was nothing in the hocus-pocus, but what a thing, I thought, to tell an eighteen-year-old boy going back into the hell of trench warfare—that he would die in a few days! Two days later my friend was dead.

Almost miraculously, I escaped not only that time but again and again, though I was severely wounded. Coming out of the hospital, I was reassigned from the Galician front lines to the Austrian army of occupation in a Ukrainian border town.

But that status was not to last long. In those historic times of 1918, armies and empires were disintegrating. I found myself deserted by my own men, completely out of touch with headquarters. The situation was hardly conducive to the long life which had been promised me, but I took what steps I could to safeguard myself.

In a peasant cart I set out for the town in which divisional headquarters were located. The route to be traveled was a dangerous one. Everywhere the country was beset by roving men, deserters tired of organized slaughter, wandering about, preaching revolution. An officer's uniform was not a recommendation for their clemency. Even more of a menace to travelers were the bandits who were picking the country's already bare skeleton.

My cart safely passed through two or three groups of foragers but finally fell into the hands of another. I was dragged from the cart into the woods. Even now I can recall the feeling of that beating. At the time I only hoped that they would continue to beat me into insensibility so that I might not feel too much if they decided to be slow and unpleasant about killing me.

They left me leaning against a tree, too tired even to hope for a quick death, as all but one of them withdrew for supper. Dimly I could feel the world about me, the fading sunlight, the dancing shadows of the leaves, the evening chirruping of the birds. I do not remember being afraid. I was not even interested, only numbly aware of discomfort.

I raised my hand to wipe a trickle of blood out of my eye. The red sun, sinking, blended with the red blood on my hand, and every line, every mark in my palm was etched in crimson. I raised my hand and stared at the outlines written in blood. From far off there came into my mind the memory of the professor's forecast of a long life. That seemed to me a wonderful joke. I looked over at the group of men sitting about their fire and no doubt at that very moment planning my death. The joke became too much for me. I laughed out loud.

My guard looked at me in amazement. He called to the leader to find out what the madman was laughing at. Slowly the bearded captain walked over and stared. I could not help it. I kept on rocking and gasping with laughter—

"Are you crazy?" asked my captor.

I explained. The joke was really too good to keep to myself. "See," I said. "It is here written that I am to live long and have much good fortune before I die." And again I went off into crazy laughter.

Suddenly a movement from the captain caught my attention. He had raised his own rough, dirt-cracked hand and was studying it curiously. Automatically, I still can't explain why, I reached over and seized his hand, turned it palm up and began to speak.

I told the ragged man a tale of greatness, of power, riches and domination. Words came fast, without thought. I soon had an audience. When the leader appeared satisfied with the glories I had found in his hand, he motioned for another to step forward and learn from my strange wisdom.

All night long in the dancing light of a small fire, I continued to look at hands and make up stories to go with them. Fatigue and everything else disappeared. I only saw hands and knew that I must keep on talking. With day, the men stopped their discussion of what I had told them and thought of food. They included me in their meal and then gathered to decide my fate. I was surprised when they offered me freedom and an escort to ensure my safety.

Certainly there was very little in this experience to convince me of there being a scientific foundation for hand analysis. My conclusion was that people were gullible, would believe anything, even take seriously the fantastic stories of a man fighting for his life. But my curiosity was aroused. Later, as roving newspaper correspondent, I had many excellent opportunities to study the hands of almost every country's outstanding personages. I determined to satisfy my curiosity.

Since then, I have collected and studied more than ten thousand handprints. As I continued, I did become more and more convinced that the hand actually showed something of a man's character, health, temperament and even his fate, at least to the extent that the last is affected by the other factors. I continued to add to my collection of handprints, feeling that the more examples I studied, the more certain I would be in my conclusions. With a larger and larger sampling to go by, I felt that I could draw some conclusions from my findings. On the basis of probabilities derived from statistical averages, I could associate certain markings in the hand with certain characteristics in men and women.

If this point of view is applied to the reading of hands, it seems to me that all the superstition and occultism of ancient palmistry can be discarded. There is then left a study which can be of great value to all sciences dealing with the study of man. Hand analysis should become a part, perhaps a very important part of the new composite study, psychobiology. The physician has already found the hands an aid in making diagnoses. In my opinion, he can make of them a very accurate index to certain ailments which manifest their symptoms in the skin, texture, nails, bones and palm of the human hand.

As for the psychologist, the study of hands provides him with a fund of information capable of being dealt. with in a thoroughly scientific manner. Best of all, the hands, in my opinion, are a bridge by means of which we can join the physician's, biologist's and physiologist's approach to his subject with that of the psychologist.

There are, for example, the endocrine glands, tiny, little-under-stood cells whose malfunctioning is registered by symptoms in the hands as well as by other physiological changes and also by profound changes in the mentality of a person, sometimes by complete shifts in personality. Physicians and psychologists recognize that attempts to change lefthandedness often lead to speech defects, mental retardation and even serious psychological maladjustments, especially in children. Daily we are adding to the evidence that hands are closely associated with all the other factors which make a human being what he is.

To the anthropologists, the study of hands should be of special interest. The various races have not only characteristic facial and cranial variations, but also marked differences in their hands. The hands of Negroes are long and narrow. The northern white races have large, broad hands. Mongolians usually have hands medium to small in size with long, sinewy fingers.

Different nationalities also tend to develop characteristic hands. The composite which is known as American is developing a hand rather longer in the fingers than that of the European nations which migrated here. The American hand has a prominent ridge across the back. The palm and fingers tend to be hard and dry. The nails are large and well shaped.

Perhaps even more than the shape of the hand, its language would interest the anthropologist. I am sure that there is a wealth of information in the gestures and motions by which men supplement their spoken language. Why are the Latins so much more expansive in their gestures than the Anglo-Saxons? What determines the different motions by which individuals express the same thing? What causes the habitual muscular response of one person or one nation to differ so markedly from another's response to the same stimulus? The answers to these questions will surely throw some light on our own origins and functionings.

I realize that this has become a long introduction, but the popular misconceptions about my subject call for much explanation. Palmistry has occupied some of the most profound minds of the past. The Chaldeans, the Assyrians and Egyptians were devotees of the art. Ancient Chinese civilizations thought that hidden meanings and occult signs could be read in the lines of the hand. Athenian philosophers have left treatises on palmistry, both Plato and Aristotle having written on the subject. Roman emperors were among its practitioners, and from ancient times to this day statesmen, kings, princes and adventurers have, before important ventures tested their luck by asking the aid of palmists.

Unfortunately the mystic and occult powers assigned to palmists almost from the beginning of time prevented study of the hands from developing into an exact science. That it is capable of being so developed I am fully convinced. I have tried in this book to approach the subject from an entirely pragmatic point of view. I have wanted to strip hand analysis of all its false trappings of mysticism. At best the subject is still a pseudo-science retaining much that is inferential rather than proven by experience. That however is unfortunately true of almost all the methods so far used in studying ourselves.

If this book succeeds at all in breaking through the superstitions which hide the true worth of hand analysis I shall feel that it has served its purpose. I should like, if nothing else, to arouse the curiosity of those who are better equipped than I to pursue the study in all its branches and implications. I feel convinced that careful scientific study of our hands has much to tell us. I look forward to the day when this will be acknowledged by all thoughtful men. Until that day, I can only hope that I have done a little to bring it nearer.

Josef Ranald

PART ONE   *Analysis and Interpretation*

Chapter I. THE VARIOUS TYPES OF HANDS AND
THEIR CHARACTERISTICS

"WHAT, will these hands ne'er be clean? Here's the smell of blood
still: all the perfumes of Arabia will not sweeten this little hand."

More truly than she knew, was the sign of murder on Lady Mac-
beth's hand. In people's hands are all their buried hopes, their
wants, their loves, their passions—the best and worst they have
ever done or ever hope to do. If you can read the stories in their
hands, you will know your friends and enemies even better than
they know themselves.

One of the few things which modern, scientific hand analysis has
retained from the lore of ancient palmistry is the classification of
human hands by their shapes. Though various students of the
hand have divided their subject into as many as 170 typical divisions,
most authorities agree on seven basic types, each with its characteristic traits.

THE ELEMENTARY HAND

The *elementary hand* belongs to the simplest and least cultivated
persons. It is easily recognized, being thick, clumsy and stolid-
looking. Its fingers are short in proportion to the palm and have a
stubby, childish appearance. The fingernails, too, have a squatty
shape. Hands like this perform the heavy labor of the world without questioning. They show little or no imagination. They do not
indicate sensitiveness to beauty, though their owners may be senti-
mentally affected by simple melodies, symbolic pictures or tender
verse.

With this elementary hand go strong family affection and prideful

9

nationalism. Emotionally, the owners of such hands are limited to simple, direct responses. The elementary hand does not show violent temper, as some authorities believe. In my experience, owners of such hands may be among the mildest and kindest of beings, though physical expression is their usual reaction to outside stimuli. Hence, the legend that they are brutal. But, actually, only certain types of elementary-handed persons, in whom jealousy or other primitive passions are easily aroused, are given to violence, and their outbursts are of the moment, rarely lasting after the first impulse has passed.

This type of hand is fast disappearing. As men improve their physical conditions and broaden their cultural interests their hands reflect the change.

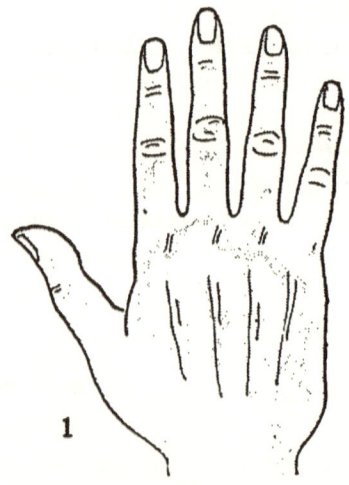

THE CONIC HAND

Today one of the most common types is the *conic*, or *sensitive* hand (see plate 1). It derives its name from its cone-like or triangular shape, broad at the base and tapering at the tip. The pure type is conically shaped both in the palm and in the fingers, each finger tapering from a wide base to a small tip. The fingertips are rounded, sometimes slightly pointed.

The conic hand is the hand of feeling, not of action. At its worst, when the palm is soft, full and without energy, it marks the introspective dreamer. It shows a vivid inner life, which may be shared with others through conversation, but rarely through activity. The conic hand usually indicates a quick mentality, an intuitive grasp of ideas, an enthusiastic responsiveness—but an interest which wanes rapidly.

People who shine in company and like to be with others often have conic hands—those who are admirably fitted for a social role, being quick, impulsive, talkative, witty and sometimes a bit malicious. They have hundreds of friendships and no friends, for they form no deep attachments. Even in love, they are inclined to be fickle. They are generous, so long as generosity requires no great effort on their part. They love luxury and comfort. They are vain, easily flattered and easily hurt.

On the finer side, people with tapering hands make up the appreciative audiences which keep our artists, poets, sculptors, painters and musicians alive. The conic hand is often called "artistic." This, I have found, gives the wrong impression. Persons with conic hands do not have the energy and force required to create beauty. They appreciate it. They enjoy it and respond to it intuitively, often without analysis or theoretical understanding.

When the conic hand is firm and full of energy, all its weaker attributes are modified, and the strong ones emphasized. Adding stability to quick understanding, such hands promise much more consistent brilliancy. The result is not only day dreams, but actual accomplishment.

THE SQUARE HAND

The *square,* or *realistic* hand (see plate 2) is almost the exact opposite of the conic. Its name describes its appearance. Palm, fingers, tips, nails—all have a squared-off, rectangular shape. To identify it, look for those indications and look especially for a straight line at the wrist and at the base of the fingers, with all the fingers attached at about the same level.

The square hand is the useful, practical, methodical hand. It usually indicates a planned life, and interests narrower than for the conic hand, but greater thoroughness and application directed in those interests. Success almost always accompanies the square hand unless other indications deny its potentialities, but achievement is

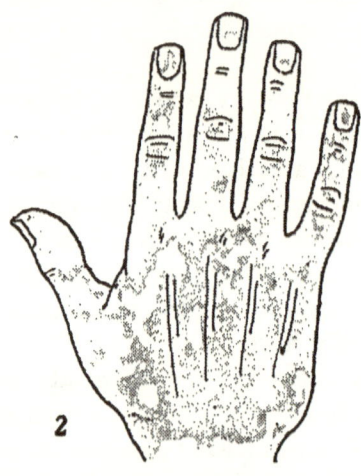

2

usually slow, through method and persistence, not through flashing brilliance. In dealing with others, squarehanded people are punctilious, slightly formal and exceedingly honest. In business, they are efficient; they have a knack of handling subordinates with impersonal fairness; and their driving force is an even, constant pressure, moving them forward. Depending on other signs in the hand, squarehanded people are capable of being either forceful executives or efficient subordinates.

But the lighter side is very much toned down in persons with realistic, square hands. The arts are studied and indulged in only if they also serve a mundane purpose, like social advancement. Squarehanded people are likely to be narrow-minded in matters outside their immediate interests. They oppose social progress, scoff at radical scientific achievement, and pooh-pooh anything which smacks of mysticism. At worst, they are dogmatic, assertive, unimaginative and domineering. At best, they are efficient, self-confident, honest and logical. Their affections rarely conflict with their worldly interests, though in family relations they are likely to be indulgent and ambitious. They have great regard for custom and tradition, though they are not easily swayed by others.

THE SPATULATE HAND

A hand which promises an interesting and active life is the *spatulate*, or *energetic* (see plate 3). It gets its name from its

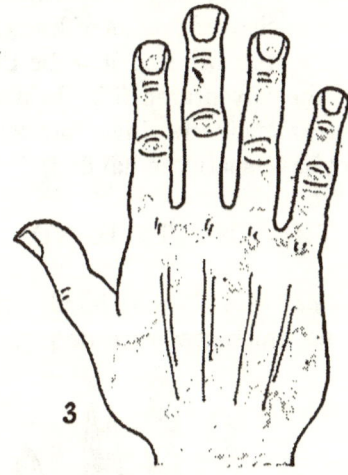

3

spready, broad fingertips and fanlike palm, shaped like the flat spatula knife which chemists use for mixing. Its palm may be broader at either the wrist or at the base of the fingers.

The outstanding attributes of a spatulate hand are driving energy, restlessness, mental and physical daring. The owners of spatulate hands are always forceful personalities, sometimes eccentric, more often just highly individualistic. They are neither credulous nor overly skeptical, approaching new ideas with enthusiasm, but applying sound reasoning.

Persons with spatulate hands tend to accept others for what they are. They have no desire to reform or to possess their friends. Consequently, their attachments may be strong, although on the surface they may appear casual. This is not fickleness in the usual sense, where like turns to dislike, love to malicious backbiting, as is sometimes true of those who have conic hands. On the contrary, the spatulate-handed are extremely loyal in friendship and cameraderie, less so in love; but shared experiences are the basis for their friendships, and parting leaves fondness without sense of loss.

The spatulate hand looks for conflict and difficulties to surmount. When it shows no humanity, its owner is likely to be tyrannical. Mussolini has such a hand, and Genghis Khan undoubtedly had. Where mental qualities are most highly developed, the spatulate hand is that of the most daring scientists, men whose quest for adventure takes them into uncharted realms of knowledge. Where physical qualities predominate, you will find it to be that of the soldier of fortune, the explorer, the adventurer. The balanced spatulate hand is usually found in great engineers, inventors and builders. Empire makers and destroyers have spatulate hands.

THE KNOTTY HAND

The *knotty* or *profound* (see plate 4) hand, also referred to as the *philosophic* hand, is one which goes with deep thought. You can rec-

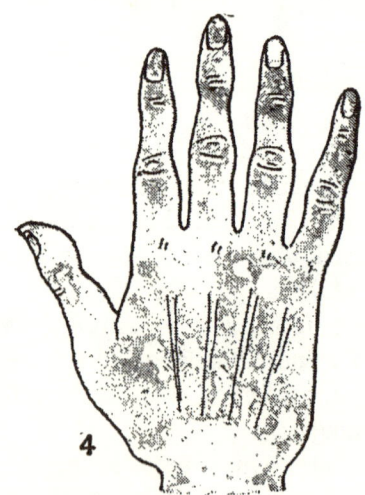

4

ognize the type by its bony structure—the joints large, the back of the hand ridged, the general outline irregular. Its fingertips are usually pointed or rounded.

Logic in its narrow sense is the outstanding trait of the knotty hand. It is the logic of abstract thought, which builds hypotheses without regard for reality, rather than the logic of practicality. The knotty-handed person delights in the intricacies of higher mathematics or metaphysical discussion. Material wellbeing is of no consequence to the owner of this philosophic hand. He is contemptuous of worldly success and is frequently almost foolhardy in generosity with his possessions. Yet he can be miserly, though unconsciously so, with himself, shutting himself into a world of his own and refusing even to recognize the travail and suffering of his neighbors. He is tolerant of all shades of opinion.

When aroused, however, the person with the profound type of hand is a fearless advocate of the rights of others. His sense of justice, his love of freedom, his contempt for meanness and cowardice place him among the bravest fighters for the rights of man.

THE POINTED HAND

The most beautiful hand is the *intuitive* or *pointed* one (see plate 5). It has the beauty of fragile porcelain, and its weakness. You will very rarely see anyone with the intuitive hand in its pure form, but many have hands so nearly approaching the type that I shall list it as one of the basic shapes. It is long and narrow, with slender, tapering fingers and long, oval, pointed nails.

The pointed hand is the hand of spiritual fervor. It goes with a trusting overcredulous nature. It has the intense emotionalism of a child, to whom everything is black as pitch one moment, radiant the next. There is no anger in this type, nor any feeling of energy or fury. Those with pointed hands are mild and forgiving, easily hurt, but easily forgetting. They are not so much illogical as without logic or cool judgment. They have no idea how to be businesslike or practical.

Yet, persons with pointed hands have a compensatory gift. What they are unable to reason out logically, they often grasp more directly. They are highly intuitive, extremely sensitive to feelings and impressions. They are attuned to receive waves or currents too delicate for other persons and even too delicate to register on the most sensitive instruments so far devised by man. For this reason, they make excellent mediums, though frequently they are unaware of their sixth sense.

Love of beauty and disgust with ugliness are often guiding principles in the lives of those who have intuitive hands. The authors of

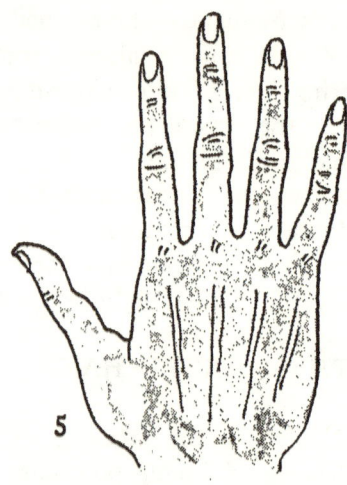

5

our most inspired lyrical poetry have often had this type of hand. They live through their feelings. Their emotions swing from ecstasy, when they are loved, to despair when they feel themselves lonely and useless.

COMBINED TYPES

Of course, there are few persons nowadays whose hands are of one type alone. Most of us are much more complex than that. There are various combinations, such as a square hand with exceptionally long, though still squaretipped fingers (see plate 6). Such a combination is an excellent one, the long fingers adding an inquiring mind and keen observation to the practical nature which goes with a purely square hand.

Knotty fingers on a square hand (see plate 7) will add mental originality, a sense of justice and daring to the qualities indicated by squareness. Spatulate fingers with a square hand give originality and energy. Such a combination is excellent for an inventor. A square hand with conic or pointed fingers is a good indication for creative art work, the square palm giving method and perseverance, the tapering fingers contributing sensitiveness and love of beauty. Even

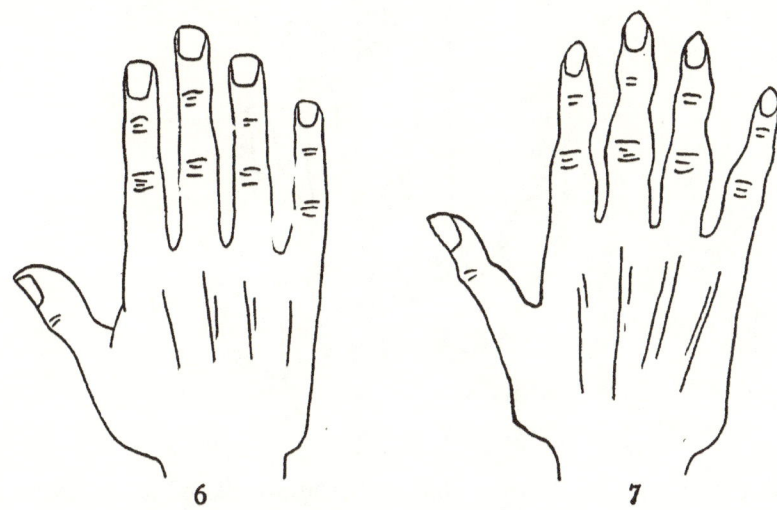

in this combination, however, the force and drive of energy are needed to make for real accomplishment.

THE MIXED HAND

More common even than a hand combining only two types is the thoroughly *mixed* or *versatile* hand (see plate 8). In this, the fingers often belong to different types, and the palm may be of still another shape, or combine characteristics of a number of different ones. The outside edge may, for example, tend to the oval, the other be rectangular.

To analyze such a hand, the student must determine what its dominant forces are. I shall discuss that in the chapter on the mounts and in the one about the fingers. Aside from what the individual fingers tell us, we can consider certain tendencies common to all mixed hands.

The mixed hand shows versatility combined with a variability of purpose which often negates the former. People with mixed hands are facile, resourceful, adaptable. They are restless and inquisitive, enthusiastic and inventive. But they often fail to develop any one of

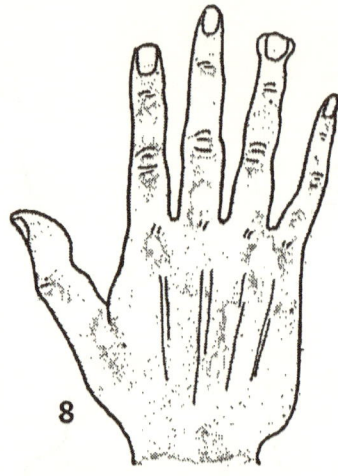

their many gifts to its limit and so become jacks of all trades and masters of none. Of course, the weaknesses in a mixed hand are lessened by energy and purpose and magnified if the will is not strong.

In studying a hand, try to classify it according to one of the seven types. If, as is most often true, you decide that your subject is of the mixed type, then determine what the dominant traits are. When the hand is so much a mixture that you cannot point to any one or two dominants, then make a careful analysis of the fingers, lines and mounts, balancing the various factors against each other.

Chapter II. THE FINGERS

SINCE most hands are of the mixed type, each finger must be considered separately. The fingers, being instruments of the brain and connected with it through the tiny telegraph wires of the nerves, represent certain qualities. Each finger indicates specific talents or failings. The size of the finger, its shape, its texture and proportions, modify the basic qualities represented by that finger.

To be considered good, fingers should be straight, in proportion to the rest of the hand, and they should be set level with each other at their bases. A low base detracts from the qualities represented by a finger. Fingers set close together indicate a formal, restrained, suspicious nature. Wide spaces show unconventionality and a free and easy trend.

In chirology, there are only four fingers (see plate 9), the thumb being so important that it is classed by itself. The index finger is called the first, or finger of Jupiter. The middle finger, the second.

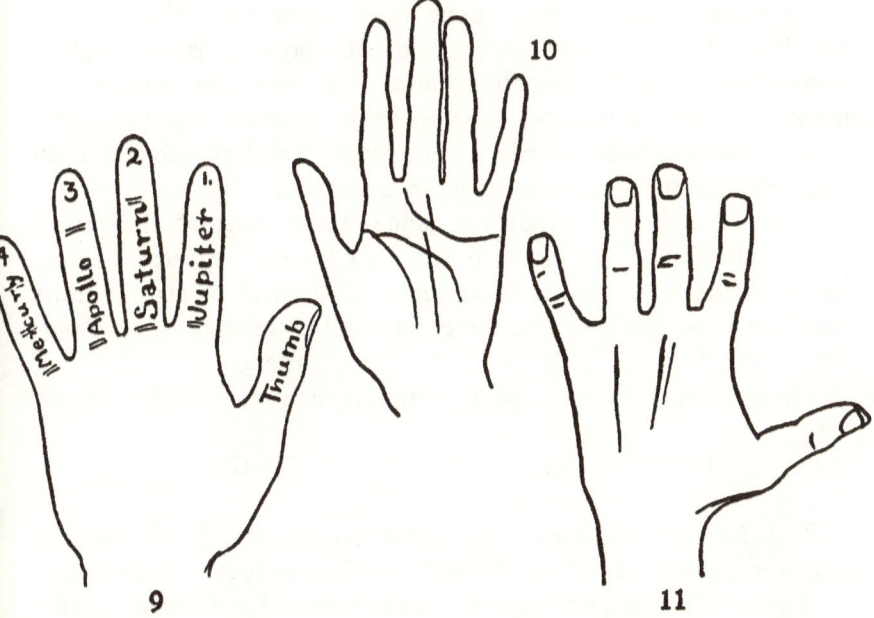

is the finger of Saturn. The ring finger, third, is the finger of Apollo. The little finger, fourth and last, is the finger of Mercury.

These names were adopted in early times. Because palmistry was associated with astrology, the four fingers received the names of planets, more remotely, of Roman gods. For convenience, I am retaining the traditional finger names, though of course I do not connect them in any way with the schematic superstitions of astrology.

LONG AND SHORT FINGERS

In studying the fingers, two important things must first be determined: whether the fingers as a whole are long (see plate 10) or short (see plate 11) and which one or two fingers are dominant ones. Length cannot be judged entirely from the relative size of the fingers and the palm, for a hand may have an unusually long palm with normal fingers, which would make the fingers appear short rather than normal. When the palm is approximately the same in width as in length, normal fingers would be about as long, reaching almost to the wrist if doubled over. Long ones would reach the wrist or even beyond it, and short ones would end above. This test cannot, however, actually be made by bending the hand, for the stiffness of the hand and its thickness, almost as much as the fingers' length, would determine how far the fingers reach. The best method is to judge the distance by eye or actual measurement.

For ideal balance, the thumb should be as long as the fourth finger and the first as long as the third. Of course, greatness rarely goes with ideal balance. It is the unusual strength of certain traits which gives us geniuses and leaders as well as crackpots and criminals. Long fingers, on the whole, indicate patience, love of detail, system and order. Short ones go with impulsiveness, action, speed.

WIDTH AND CONTOUR OF FINGERS

Thick fingers are the practical, materialistic ones. When they are very thick, they show love of luxury and a tendency towards self-indulgence. Thin fingers may show indulgence of a different kind—petulance and worry—for thin fingers are exacting and nervous. As to the contours, smoothness—when the joints do not protrude—indicates an open, frank, company-loving nature, light-hearted, talkative and somewhat shallow. Knotty joints go with seriousness, thought and mental self-sufficiency.

FLEXIBILITY

Whether the fingers are flexible or stiff is extremely significant. Firm fingers show an intense, passionate, violent nature, one which might accomplish great things individually or as a leader, but which cannot cooperate with others or work as a subordinate. The drawbacks of such fingers are intolerance, stubbornness and lack of tact.

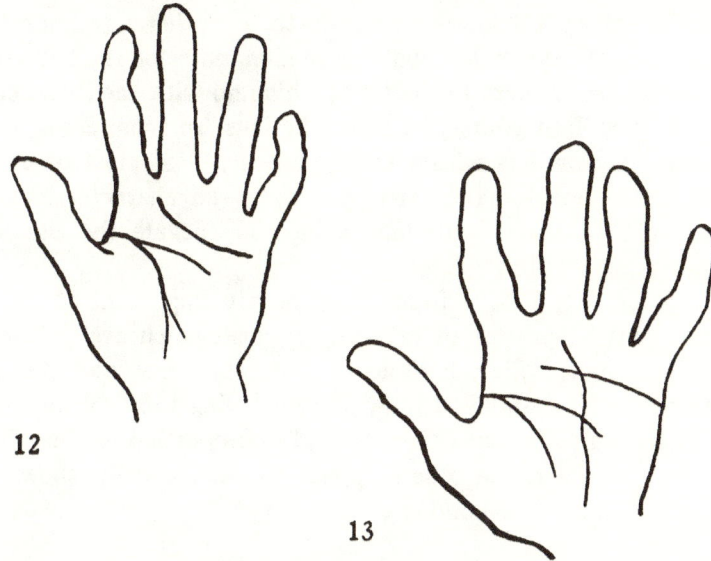

12

13

The last is especially pronounced when the fingers are short as well as stiff.

With flexibility goes an intensification of the qualities of the mount and finger. Supple fingers indicate adaptability, tact, wit and success in social contacts, though not necessarily a love of company.

CROOKED FINGERS

Crooked fingers (see plate 12) show distortion or misuse of the qualities which go with the misshapen finger, but the knotty, bony structure of the profound hand should not be confused with bent or crooked shape. Nor is crookedness the same as a slight bending to one side. Fingers bent laterally (see plate 13) always emphasize shrewdness, and this indication should be studied in conjunction with the particular qualities ascribed to the finger having such a bend. A finger twisted on its axis exaggerates the moral or physical defects associated with that finger.

DOMINANT FINGERS

In most persons, the fingers differ greatly from each other in length, smoothness, thickness, and so forth. It is therefore important not only to determine which qualities predominate for the hand as a whole, but to relate them to the traits which go with each particular finger. There will, of course, be contradictions. In some cases, these indicate actual conflicts within the personality—for most of us are complex, made up of many warring desires and characteristics. In other cases, a dominant trait may completely negate the signposts of an opposing quality.

For that reason, I have found it extremely important to decide, quite early in the process of an analysis, just which are the dominant characteristics. Size, both length and thickness, and the general contours of a hand will indicate which finger is the dominant one. A finger which is larger than normal in proportion to the others, or one toward which the others appear to lean, usually shows the dominant influence in a hand.

THE PHALANXES

But before considering the fingers individually, I want to discuss the divisions of the fingers, that is, the three joints or phalanxes. The nail phalanx is always referred to as the first (see plate 14, the joints marked A); the middle division as the second (see plate 14, the joints marked B); the one nearest the palm, the third (see plate 14, the joints marked C). I have found that you can divide the phalanxes roughly, classing the first (A) in each finger as indicator of mental qualities, the second (B), of practical and business qualities, the third (C) as guide to physical qualities.

It is my experience that persons with long first phalanxes are most active in the mental field. When the second phalanx is longest and largest, the practical and business side will be uppermost. When the third phalanx leads, I have found the subject greatly absorbed in the physical side of life.

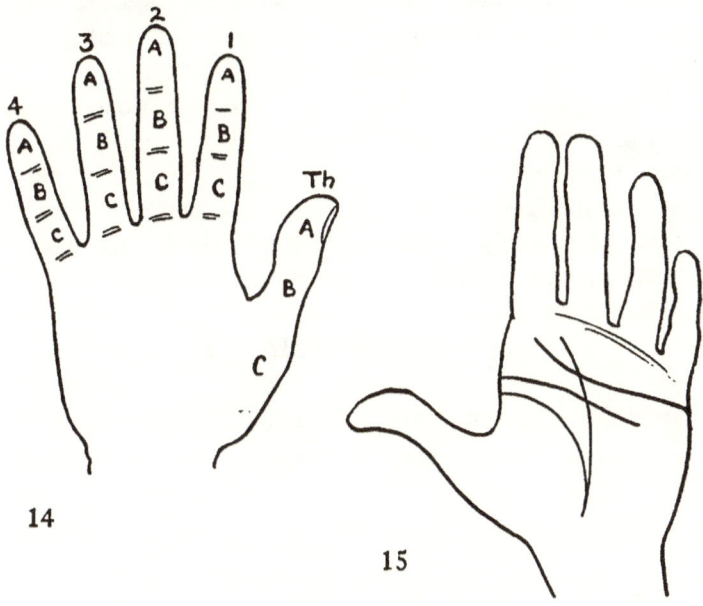

14

15

THE JUPITER FINGER

The first finger, Jupiter (see plate 9), indicates ambition, love of power, pride, leadership and also devoutness. When this finger is the dominant one (see plate 15), some or all these qualities will, in varying degree, be strong motivations. When the finger is very inflexible, cruelty and tyranny may be added to the qualities of leadership. If the Jupiter finger is hooked, the ambition will be a selfish one, and the owner of such a finger may not be overscrupulous in his choice of means. A very thin and nervous index finger, even though long, does not mean purposeful ambition or leadership. Rather does it indicate the frustrated wish for power, realized only in day-dreams.

Of course, the first phalanx and the fingertip modify the general meaning of a long first finger. A pointed tip on the first finger denotes intuition especially if the inside surface is very full; square tip shows love of truth; a spatulate one, bigotry; an oval one, refinement. When the nail phalanx is long, intuition is again emphasized; while a short first phalanx indicates the skeptic. Thickness of Jupiter's first phalanx implies sensual qualities, and a thin nail phalanx on the first finger indicates austere rigidity.

The middle phalanx when long shows determination; lack of energy when it is short; selfishness when it is thick; and honors, rather than riches, as the spur of ambition, when this phalanx is thin.

A long base phalanx on the index finger is a sign of love of power; a short one, of modesty and resignation. Thickness here shows sensuality or gluttony; slenderness, control of the appetites.

THE SATURN FINGER

The second, or Saturn finger as the middle finger is called (see plate 9), governs thought. When this finger is the dominant one (see

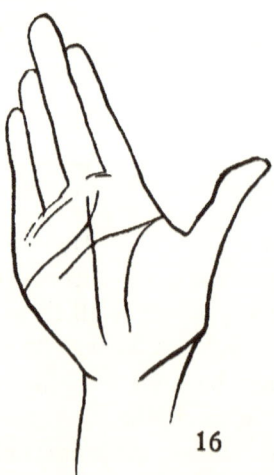

16

plate 16), towering above its two neighbors, our subject is likely to be serious and given to solitude. He may have humor, but it is probably of a satiric nature. A weak second finger, whether unusually short or abnormally thin, shows frivolity or lack of concentration.

If the nail phalanx of the Saturn finger (see plate 14, 2A) is long and tapering, we can be sure of a cautious, persistent and sincere personality. If the tip is pointed, look for lightness. When it is square, expect a serious person with sound judgment. A spatulate tip on the Saturn finger shows the pessimist. A short first phalanx indicates the fatalist; a thick one, carelessness; a very thin one, cruelty.

The middle phalanx on the Saturn finger (see plate 14, 2B), when long, shows precision and a scientific approach; when short the opposite—credulity and a mystical bent. Thick, it goes with great physical energy and capacity for manual labor; thin, with philosophic logic and exactness.

A long base phalanx on the middle finger (see plate 14, 2C) indicates love of solitude; a short one, lack of control in giving—either meanness or overgenerosity. This phalanx, if thick, shows a materialistic and plodding temperament; if thin, it indicates miserliness. Thus, a short, thin base phalanx on the Saturn finger would certainly indicate meanness rather than overgenerosity.

THE APOLLO FINGER

The third finger, that of Apollo (see plate 9), governs sociability, the arts, and self-esteem. To have this finger dominant is an excellent sign for actors, singers, and those who seek careers in the applied arts. The top phalanx in this finger (see plate 14, 3A) has a great variety of connotations, depending on its size and shape. Bent back, it indicates appreciation of beauty. This appreciation takes on a formal quality when the phalanx is thin, a hint of sensuality if it is thick. A pointed tip on the Apollo finger signifies a tendency towards mysticism and a clinging to false values in judgment. A short phalanx shows simplicity; a long one, eccentricity, a seeking after queer, sometimes unattainable objectives. With an oval tip, I have usually found ease in speech, sometimes lack of discretion. A square tip shows a positive, certain nature; a spatulate one energy and activity.

The middle phalanx in the Apollo finger (see plate 14, 3B) is extremely important for those in creative fields, for it shows creative ability when it is long—and lack of aesthetic sensibility when it is short. Thickness goes with originality.

The base phalanx of the Apollo finger (see plate 14, 3C) indicates the realist if it is short, the coxcomb if it is long. Thickness in this phalanx bespeaks a sense of dramatics and a love of color; a thin, waisted shape, indifference, lack of enthusiasm.

THE MERCURY FINGER

The fourth, or little finger, which is called the finger of Mercury (see plate 9), governs business abilities and the faculty of speech, whether written or oral. The tip of this finger shows inventiveness and restlessness, an active and resourceful nature, when it has a spatulate shape; common sense, when it is square; a visionary, metaphysical strain, when it is pointed; and refinement, a formal sense of values, when it is oval. If Mercury's top phalanx is hooked, it indicates a self-centered, not overscrupulous person; and when it is bent back, you will find someone who is inquisitive and talkative. Length in this phalanx shows love of study, though usually study of a practical nature. Shortness indicates mental laziness. Thickness is a sign of lack of delicacy.

A very thin middle phalanx in the little finger (see plate 14, 4B) gives us the gambler, or a very ambitious person who is impatient of the usual methods of fulfilling his ambitions. A long middle phalanx indicates a commercial or legal bent. A short middle phalanx shows loyalty.

When the base phalanx of the Mercury finger (see plate 14, 4C) is long, look for eloquence and cunning; when it is short, a straightforward, credulous nature. If this phalanx is thick, you have an indication of sex complexes; thin, of a precise, analytical mind.

HOW TO INTERPRET THE FINGERS

The fingers, indicating as they do the special talents and aptitudes of the person you are studying, are most important in applying hand analysis to vocational guidance or training. The indications of the fingers must, however, be read in conjunction with the information revealed by the hand as a whole and by the lines and markings in the palm. For example, when a very long base on the finger of Mercury, the little finger, indicates eloquence and cunning, and you find that other signs show a timid, retiring nature, you may be sure you have a potential demagogue, but one who is likely to remain anonymous, appealing through the written word, or possibly making no use at all of his gift of eloquence. Thus, the various contradictory evidences must be balanced against one another. You should accept as keynotes to the personality you are studying only the strong traits or those which are consistently indicated throughout the entire hand.

Chapter III. THE THUMB

WHEN Professor G. Elliot Smith identified the few fragments of bone which are all that remains of the Peking Man as definitely those of a very early human being, and not of an ape, he based his classification on the hand, especially the thumb. More than any other member, the thumb marks man as different from the beasts. If you want the secret of what distinguishes the leader, the creator, the successful and influential man from his fellows, likely as not, you will find that secret in his thumb.

Notice how short and rigid are the thumbs on plate 17, showing handprints made by an anthropoid ape. In the hand of man, the thumb is opposable, that is, it can swing in an arc and touch every one of the other fingers. An ape's thumb cannot. Our manual dexterity, our ability to handle tools, to create, to build, to write, to guide fine instruments, we owe to our thumbs.

LARGE AND SMALL THUMBS

The thumb, unlike the fingers which tell of specific talents, governs the general qualities of will, reason and appetites. Therefore, the thumb and fingers must be considered together, for the thumb will usually tell what use we put our gifts to. A large thumb strengthens the qualities of weak fingers, deficient in energy and practicality. It also emphasizes those qualities in a hand already having energy and will, perhaps to an extent which may be brutalizing. A large thumb

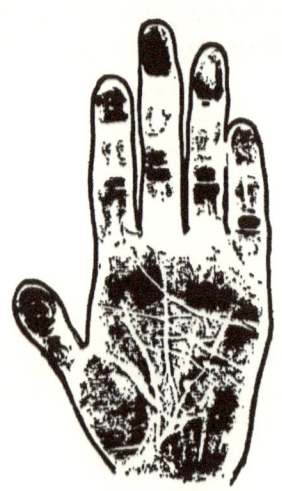 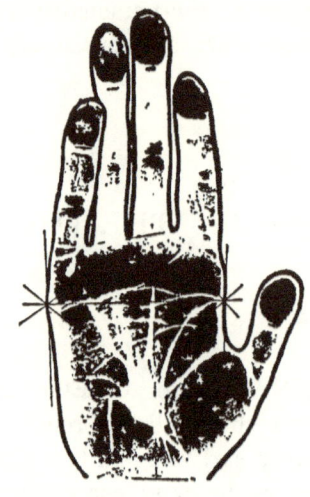

17

adds quickness and determination to the practicality of short fingers. A small thumb negates the force of such hands. A large thumb is excellent with long fingers, for it bolsters their method and thoughtfulness. A small thumb makes the long-fingered person fussy and irritable, conscious of small details but unwilling or unable to work methodically.

Conic or pointed fingertips with a small thumb show artistic feeling but no creative power. Add a large thumb to such fingers, and you are likely to have a poet or artist. Large thumbs increase the power and energy of spatulate tips and give direction and purpose to square hands. Small thumbs always detract from the positive qualities of a hand, not so much by lessening the talents as by interfering with their application.

The normal thumb, when held straight up along the side of the hand, should reach to about the middle of the index finger's base phalanx (see plate 18), and its second and third phalanx should be of equal size.

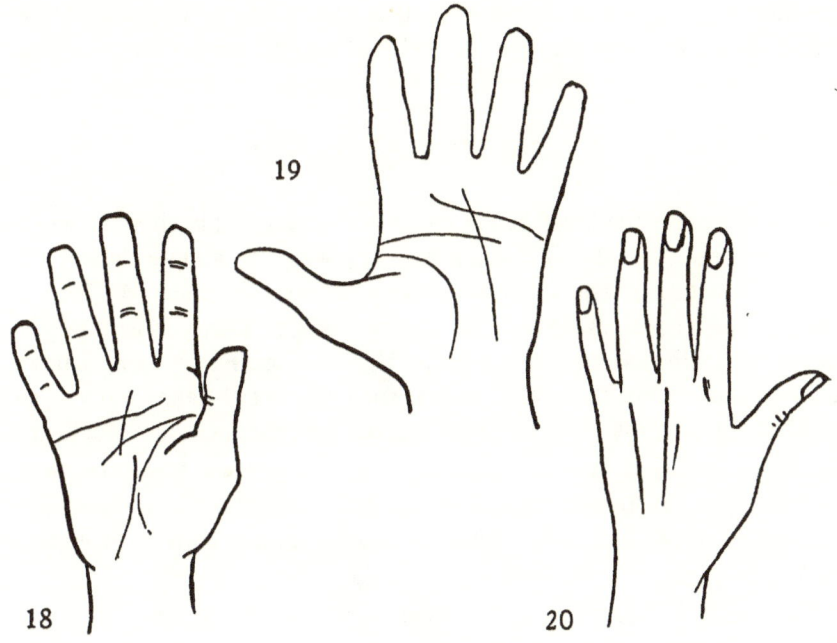

19

18   20

THE THUMB'S SETTING

Of course, the relative height of the thumb measured by the first finger differs with the setting of the thumb—whether high or low on the hand. Often a low-set thumb, even when it is long, will reach only to the base of the first finger.

The lower on the side of the hand the origin of the thumb, the greater the intelligence, as a rule. When the thumb is set low (see plate 19), it is able to move in a wide, sweeping arc, indicating a generous, liberty-loving, independent and sympathetic person. When the thumb is high-set (see plate 20), especially if it is held close to the hand, you will find a secretive, cautious and timid disposition. If the thumb is set very close to the hand and appears inflexible, you can expect meanness and suspicion; but if the other aspects of the hand are good, the close setting may indicate only lack of self-confidence, shyness and oversensitiveness. This is particularly so in persons who normally hide their thumbs in the half-closed palm. A medium setting of the thumb with free movement at the side of the hand indicates a person who is well balanced, neither extravagant nor mean, neither obstinate nor weak-willed; frank, honest and loyal.

THE THUMB'S PHALANXES

In the thumb the three phalanxes have very specific significance—the first (see plate 14, TH-A) governing will, the second (see plate 14, TH-B) reason and logic, the base phalanx (see plate 14, TH-C) feeling and appetites. When the first, or will phalanx, is excessively developed, stiff and very much larger than the second phalanx, I have usually found an obstinate person with a violent temper and the need to impose his own will and desires on others. A more delicate tip on a highly-developed will-phalanx modifies its brutality with sensitiveness. A broad, spatulate tip increases the force, brutality and strength. A square tip gives us a very unimaginative, stubborn person, a fanatic in his own narrow way.

When the will-phalanx is too short in proportion to the rest of the thumb, we can expect weak will, a person easily influenced by others and falling for every temptation. A pointed or tapering end on a short will-phalanx indicates almost hopeless weakness. A forceful tip on a short will-phalanx diminishes the weakness.

THE PHALANX OF REASON

The second thumb phalanx (see plate 14, TH-B) governs perception, judgment and reasoning powers. If long, it gives the ability to plan to make decisions, to use sound judgment. When a long second phalanx is combined with a short will-phalanx, you find a person who can make intricate plans but falls short in their execution. On the other hand, a deficient phalanx of reason with strong will, leads to action which may often be foolish or misapplied. Waisted formation of the phalanx of reason goes with an ability to make fine distinctions.

THE BASE PHALANX OF THE THUMB

The base phalanx of the thumb (see plate 14, TH-C) governs affection and the senses. When this section is long, these attributes are strong, and, if the phalanx is at the same time thin, the passions will be under control. Fleshiness in this portion of the hand indicates self indulgence, egotism, love of domination, and a tendency to exploit others. A normal development of the thumb's base phalanx gives us well-balanced control, an affectionate disposition, and a sense of fairplay.

CHARACTERISTIC SHAPES OF THE THUMB

There are many very distinct variations in the shape of the thumb. With the elementary hand, we usually find an almost shapeless thumb, heavy, short and coarse. With this thumb, we will usually discover little intelligence or control, and a coarse brutality.

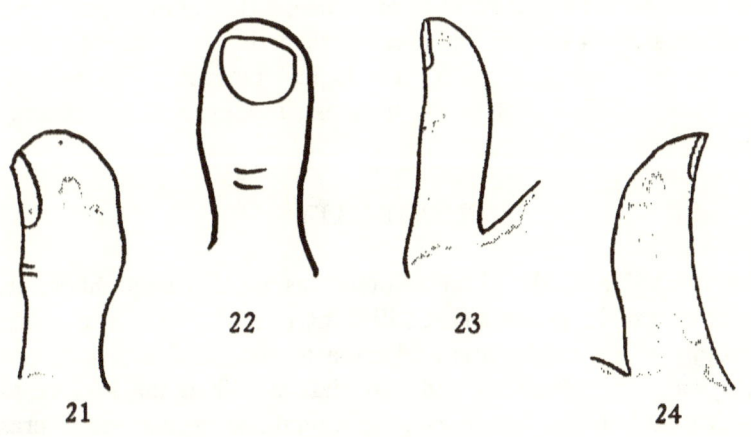

21   22   23   24

The *club-shaped* thumb (see plate 21) has a heavy, ball-shaped will-phalanx, thick and round, with a short nail of rough texture. This shape assures tremendous obstinacy and, in a hand which is otherwise of low grade, a violent temper. Because of its association with violence, the club-shaped thumb has been called the "murderer's thumb," though of course it does not actually indicate a murderer. In fact, the violent characteristics linked to it may be completely submerged and never given expression.

In nervous persons, I have often found the thumb quite flat, as though spread out by a weight and usually soft and flabby in texture.

A thumb which has a broad structure and firm, healthy texture tells of determination backed by aggressiveness and physical strength. I have frequently found thumbs of this type on the hands of highly successful men.

When the will-phalanx is broad on the nail side and spread out into a paddle-like shape (see plate 22), you have strong determination, which, if over-developed, becomes tyranny and obstinacy. The paddle shape gives strength even if the phalanx is flat from front to back, though in that case the strength may be only mental control with low physical endurance.

A very long and slender thumb indicates sensitiveness, accompanied by great power of will, excellent reasoning ability, and intuitional understanding.

The ideal for a normal hand is, of course, a thumb of normal length and thickness, well-shaped and evenly proportioned. It shows strength of will as well as the capacity for logical reasoning. With such a thumb, you will find diplomacy, firmness, intelligence, and discrimination.

FLEXIBILITY

The flexibility of the thumb, almost as much as its shape, tells the character of its possessor. A stiff joint (see plate 23) which holds the thumb in a straight line and close to the hand indicates practicality, caution, reliability and materialism. When the texture and shape of a stiff thumb are coarse, these qualities degenerate to crassness.

A flexible thumb (see plate 24), bending outward at the joint, shows an extravagant, open-hearted, adventurous nature. Emotional exuberance, brilliant social qualities, adaptability and wit go with this supple thumb. To make for happiness, these fortunate qualities should, however, be checked by practicality and self-reliance.

In studying a hand, always balance the indications of the thumb with the traits shown by the fingers and palm. A strong thumb on a sensitive, weak hand may supply the force needed to bring complete realization of the self. A weak thumb may negate all the gifts of a brilliant personality.

Chapter IV. THE PALM

THE palm itself, its shape and consistency, aside from the markings upon it, tells much about the person whose hand you are studying. Development of the hand, which is the instrument of the brain, is dependent on all the biological and chemical factors which also determine the personality. Studies of the ductless glands have given us some understanding of the complicated chemistry governing human energy, sex, and nervous reactions, from the simplest reflex to involved inhibitions and neuroses.

This same machinery of nerve communication and glandular secretions, which decides the weight, height and nervous and muscular responses of the individual, also determines the development of the hand. From studying a large number of hands, I have been able to associate particular types of palmar structure with specific characteristics.

For example, the consistency of the hand tells much about the individual. A firm, full, elastic palm, warm and alive to the touch, indicates a person who is active, well-directed, alive. Flabbiness shows a phlegmatic disposition, to which action comes with an effort. If the palm is at the same time both flabby and covered with minute lines, you may be sure that the subject dissipates his energies in nervous reactions. If the palm is thick, flabby and soft, indolence, whether physical or mental, is indicated, and the fleshier such a soft hand, the greater will be the love of ease and luxury.

When the palm is thin and narrow, you can expect a narrow, timid individual, lacking mental ability and moral force. A person with this sort of palm is likely to be shallow and selfish. When the fingers on a narrow palm are long, tyranny on a small scale—restricted to personal relations—is indicated. A palm with high eminences shows a warm, responsive nature. A flat surface usually goes with intellectual interests.

If the palm is in good proportion to the fingers, about the same in length and width, and if it is even in shape, firm, though not hard, it shows a well-balanced, receptive mind, control of the emotions, intelligent use of the talents. When the palm is overdeveloped in relation to the fingers, I have usually found the individual over-confident and egocentric. If the palm's development is especially heavy at the base, near the wrist, sensuality is indicated. A hand which is particularly heavy at the wrist and at the same time hard in consistency shows brutality unless a strong but sensitive thumb or an exceptionally good headline (see plate 27) negatives this indication.

THE HOLLOW PALM

A hollow palm shows lack of aggressiveness and perseverance. It is frequently associated with misfortune. Undoubtedly, the lack of these qualities is the cause of much ill luck and for that reason poor development in the center of the hand must be regarded as an ill omen, no matter how favorable the rest of the hand may be.

The depression in the center of the hand often lies in the direction of a particular line or section of the palm, and then it specifically relates to the faculties associated with the line, mount, or sign toward which the hollow inclines. When the hollow falls under the line of life, I have sometimes found it to be an indication of domestic troubles; when under the line of destiny, it is associated with disappointment in connection with one's career.

LARGE AND SMALL HANDS

The size of the hand as a whole is of extreme importance. The legend that large hands are capable, I have found from experience to be little more than a superstition. Usually, a large hand, particularly if long-fingered, will be methodical and inclined towards detail work. But the hands which go with the conception of large projects, with the formulation of breath-taking plans, with discovery, daring and forceful execution, are comparatively small. Large hands need direction from others. Small hands supply the direction.

LEFT AND RIGHT HAND

Since most changes in the hand resulting from growth of the personality and adjustment to circumstances manifest themselves in the palm, I am going to discuss the significance of the left and right hands in conjunction with the palm, rather than in connection with the hand as a whole.

The right hand is the one to study in a right-handed person. That hand gives us a picture of the human being as he is. The left hand tells us what he might have been—whether for better or worse. What the left hand pictures is a person's inheritance, the weaknesses, the strength, the talents and the lacks with which he was born. From the left hand we are able to judge a person's potentialities. From the right what he has created out of his potentialities. In a left-handed person, the significance of the two hands is of course reversed.

This sort of knowledge is a weapon, and with knowledge of our weaknesses we may be able to overcome them. Here is one very great value in the message of the left hand. By pointing out the pitfalls into which we are likely to fall, it helps us to avoid them.

In the right hand we see how far we have developed or dissipated our inherent endowments. Frequently you will find the two hands very different from each other. Sometimes, especially in hands with weak thumbs, you will see all the vices and pitfalls, the illnesses, the lacks hinted at in the hand of inheritance confirmed and magnified in the hand of actuality. In persons of strong will you will find the opposite—a tendency to flightiness bolstered by purpose, wayward emotions held in check by reason.

It is therefore important, in studying the hands, to compare the general contours of the palms, the left with the right. Examine each of the mounts to see whether they differ in prominence in the two hands. Look with special care at the principal lines of the hands. Of all the hand's markings, the lines are the most sensitive to changes taking place in a person. As you grow or shrink in mental stature, your line of head will reflect the change. It will also register your mental health. I have seen hands in which a naturally vivid imagination was allowed to atrophy until the right hand showed not a trace of this gift but, instead, had a level, extremely matter-of-fact line of head. The left hand, at the same time, retained a low-dipping line of head which testified to the original bent.

The same applies to the line of heart. In persons who have had to repress affectionate responsiveness, I have often found the line of heart in the right hand growing faint and narrow, sometimes diverted out of its original course to show the influence of self-seeking instead of generosity.

The line of destiny may, in the left hand, be almost destroyed by obstacles. But in the right hand it may be remade, showing the conquest of difficulties by a strong person. Unfortunately, the reverse is just as often true. Failure to make use of natural gifts, wasted energy, misdirected ambitions leave their imprint in a broken or abruptly ended line of destiny.

In any case, the message of the operative hand is never a static one. Comparison of the two hands tells us where we have gone astray from the path which would have been best for us, and it is thus possible to correct our mistake.

Of course, in a lefthanded person, the readings have to be reversed. Just what the cause of lefthandedness or ambidexterity is we do not know. It is, however, a recognized fact that the tendency to use one hand rather than the other is closely associated with the balance of the central nervous system. Changing the balance by forcing a naturally lefthanded person to use his right is likely to have disastrous results. Many speech defects are laid to interference with the natural dominance of one hand or the other.

In children especially, nervous maladjustment, extreme shyness and slow perception result from trying to make them use the right hand when the left is the naturally operative. Formerly schools and parents tried to make left-handed youngsters learn penmanship and other manual arts with the right hand. Nowadays advanced educators have learned that difficult behavior problems, secretiveness, lying, even stealing, result from such interference with nature's intentions. Parents and teachers should be especially careful about trying to readjust a child's natural preference for one hand or the other.

Chapter V. THE MOUNTS OF THE HAND AND THEIR ATTRIBUTES

WHEN you look at the inner face of the palm, you do not see a flat surface, like a table top, but instead you find many small and large muscular swellings. If you study their formation carefully you will notice that there is such a pad under each finger and that there are others toward the wrist and in the center of the palm.

These swellings are known as the mounts of the hand. The mounts under the fingers take their names from the individual fingers and in general share the qualities ascribed to their corresponding finger: thus, mount Jupiter lies under the index finger; mount Saturn under the second finger; mount Apollo under the ring finger; and Mount Mercury under the finger of Mercury. The two mounts of Mars, known as Mars positive and Mars negative, are located under the mounts of Jupiter and Mercury, respectively. The large mounts at the base of the palm are Luna on the outer edge and Venus forming the base of the thumb. Plate 25 shows the positions of the mounts of the hand.

MOUNT JUPITER

The mount of Jupiter, underneath the first finger, indicates pride and ambition, the desire to dominate others. When mount Jupiter is well developed and the finger of Jupiter is dominant, you will find pride swollen into vanity and bluster.

The Jupiterian—one in whom the finger of Jupiter is dominant and the mount highly developed—is frequently religious and derives great comfort from the pageantry and show of church worship. You will often find high dignitaries of the church among the children of Jupiter.

Of course, the qualities of leadership which go with a strong finger of Jupiter can also find their expression in other fields. For example,

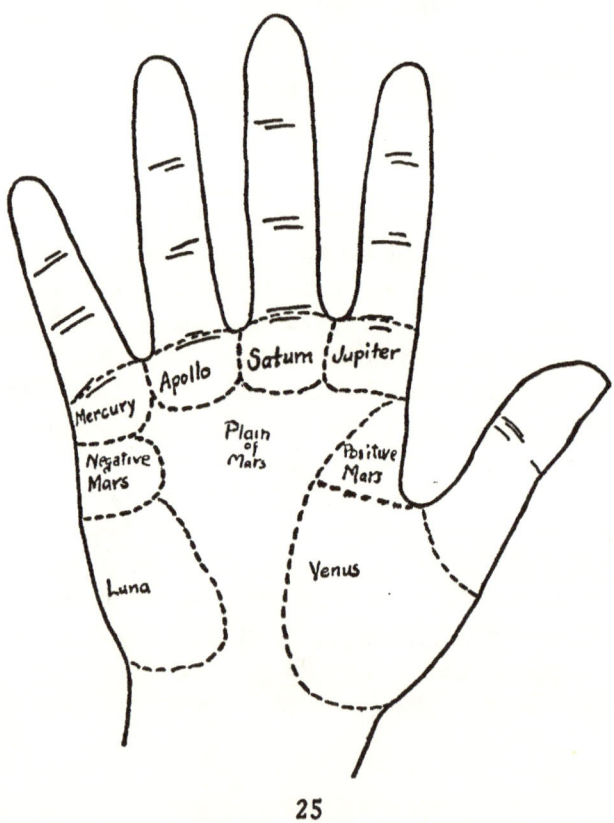

25

given long spatulate-tipped fingers and a domineering thumb, your Jupiterian might well be a military conqueror, his qualities being orderliness and rigidity, ambition, energy and daring, and a desire to dominate others.

MOUNT SATURN

The mount of Saturn under the second finger signifies seriousness, thought, and prudence, especially in money matters. I have rarely seen very strong development of this mount together with a strong finger of Saturn. In fact, the mount is sometimes depressed when the finger shows strength. However, even when the mount is not very prominent, a person may still be classified as a Saturnian if the second finger is dominant.

When the Saturn finger has slender, waisted phalanxes, the thoughtful mind is accentuated. Credulity will be reduced to a minimum, and you have a critical, skeptical, analytical brain. The Saturnian distrusts others until he has satisfied himself of their motives. Consequently, he is usually an individualist, undertaking business enterprises by himself and disliking unnecessary social contacts. This is fortunate for the others as much as for himself, because the Saturnian is dour and pessimistic, a wet blanket on the exuberance of those who have a different temperament.

The thrift which characterizes the Saturnian is exaggerated into meanness and miserliness if the lowest (material) phalanx is strongest. And if the heart line is unstable and the tip of a dominant Saturn finger unusually sensitive, you have a morbid cast to the thoughts with a tendency toward self-criticism and despondency.

MOUNT APOLLO

The mount of Apollo, like the mount of Jupiter, shows ambition, but it is a more highly specialized ambition—for renown and admiration. This finger and mount have almost the exact opposite connotation from that of Saturn. The Apollonian looks for success and self-realization through other people. He is gay, sociable, worldly, emotional. He is a lover of beauty, though not a creator of it.

When the third finger is excessively long and the mount well developed, impulsiveness is exaggerated to the point of rashness, and the owner of such a hand is likely to be fascinated by gambling. A long space between the base of the thumb and of the first finger emphasizes this tendency still further.

The Apollonian may be an excellent business man. For confirmation, look to a long middle phalanx on the Apollo finger, and a good line of head. Likely as not, this type of Apollonian will display his love of drama, beauty and color in some way through his business activities.

The bad qualities of the mount and finger of Apollo predominate if the finger is crooked, or if the mount or base phalanx is excessively developed in comparison with the other two. Then the subject will be vain, boastful, reckless, and perhaps sexually vicious or dissolute. But, on the whole, the mount of Apollo introduces optimism and gaiety into life, acting an an antidote to the heaviness of Saturn.

MOUNT MERCURY

Quickness is the quality most associated with the mount of Mercury under the fourth finger. The Mercurian has a keen, almost intuitive mind, especially if the Apollo mount is at the same time fairly well developed. He is exceedingly shrewd, and, if he has a bad hand, or if the finger itself is twisted or shows only worldly tendencies, his active brain is likely to hatch cunning schemes for the exploitation of his fellows. The Mercurian is never a brutally vicious type, but rather a gyp artist or con man, shyster lawyer or promoter of fraudulent enterprises. If all the fingers are crooked with a highly developed mount of Mercury, you have definite indication of a criminal type of mind.

Unlike the Saturnian, whose analytical mind finds difficulty in expressing itself, the Mercurian is gifted with an easy flow of words. He makes an excellent trial lawyer, a brilliant advocate, though more likely moved to speak by ambition than by devotion to the cause he is championing.

MOUNT LUNA

The Mount of Luna, at the base of the palm on its outer side, governs the imagination and intuition. Good development of this mount plus directed energy are necessary to transform the Apollonian, with his appreciation of art, into the creator. And, with a well developed finger and mount of Mercury, a prominent mount of Luna gives promise of creative ability to writers of fiction and romance.

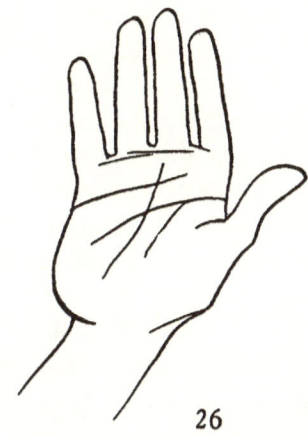

26

The kind of fingertips and thumb combined with a well-developed mount of Luna are extremely important, for, with a weak, oversensitive hand, the imagination is wasted in dreaming. When practicality is lacking, the mount of Luna may lead to activity, but of a fantastic nature, such as the designing of machines of perpetual motion, to choose an extreme example.

To judge whether mount Luna is well developed, examine its bulge both along the side of the hand and upward from the surface of the palm. A well-rounded curve on the outer edge of the hand indicates good development. If the mount is both outcurving and high, the mount of Luna can be classed as very strong. (See plate 26.) Vertical lines on this mount add to its strength. Crosswise markings weaken it, or indicate defects such a morbid trend to the imagination.

Mount Luna should always be studied in connection with the line of head, for any inclination of the headline downwards, towards the mount of Luna, shows the influence of imagination in the thinking. In addition, signs of mental disturbances found on the line of head are often repeated or explained by the mount of Luna. Where the development of Luna is excessive, you can expect mental or emotional unbalance, or both.

MOUNT VENUS

The mount of Venus is at the base of the thumb bounded by the arc of the life line. This mount indicates both the vitality and general health of the subject and the nature of his affections. When you have a well-developed, prominent swelling on the mount of Venus, you may be sure of a generous, warm-hearted, lively personality with strong amorous instincts. Attractiveness for the opposite sex almost always goes with a well-developed mount of Venus, and health, optimistic spirits, gaiety and love of music are other attributes which belong to this type.

If the mount of Venus is overdeveloped, particularly at its base close to the wrist, the animal instincts and passions predominate. Their expression, however, is a natural one, and neither vicious nor perverted.

THE THREE MOUNTS OF MARS

The mount of Mars is the most difficult of all to study, for it is made up of three sections: Mars positive under Jupiter, above the mount of Venus; Mars negative under Mercury, above the mount of Luna; and the plain of Mars in the center of the palm (see plate 25). Each of these divisions has its own significance, though the characteristics of Mars as a whole are courage and aggressiveness.

Mars positive, near the thumb, is the most pugnacious, spirited section. Its bravery is the courage of the soldier and adventurer, which is largely physical. Mars negative, horizontally on a level with the positive Mars, but on the opposite side of the palm, is the courage of resistance. It may find expression physically, or through great moral stamina. A person with both these mounts well developed will push himself over all obstacles and never give in to defeat.

A prominent development of the plain of Mars emphasizes the traits of both Mars negative and positive. In addition, especially when the plain is crossed by many horizontal lines, it indicates violent temper. The combination becomes dangerous when there is very high development of all three portions, as temper is then immediately translated into physical violence. A strong thumb and line of head are needed to curb the impetuosity of this combination.

The triple mount of Mars has greater importance than merely to indicate courage or the lack of it, for when Mars in all its aspects is deficient, the subject is extremely weak, defeated in life even before he begins. If the morbid tendencies of Saturn are highly developed, and you find signs of an introspective imagination together with a failure in Mars, then you have a typical would-be suicide.

Apart from their significance in themselves, the mounts of the hand are important in relation to the lines of the palm. Deflections of the line of head or heart, for example, toward any one of the mounts, show the influence of that mount over the faculty with which the line is associated. For that reason, it is extremely important that a serious student of the hands be acquainted with the attributes allied to the mounts.

Chapter VI. THE LINES OF THE PALM

IN the superstitious, fortune-telling uses of palmistry, the lines of the hand are regarded as a sort of key to the future, the various directions and signs being given somewhat arbitrary significance. This point of view I have entirely discarded. I have found no basis at all in my studies of thousands of hands for the declaration that given signs definitely foretell events in the lives of men and women.

What I have found is that the human hand, connected to the brain by thousands of sensory and motor nerves, registers on its surface a kind of summary of all the messages which pass through the brain. Thus, the hand gives us an index to the personality.

There is another notion I wish to dispel. The amateur in chirology is usually of the impression that activity makes for many minute lines. This is incorrect. Undirected and wasted nervous energy cause those myriad purposeless little lines which weave over the surface of some hands. The man or woman whose activity is purposeful and useful usually has a few, well-defined markings telling the entire story. But the marked absence of lines is indication, not of concentration in activity, but of a phlegmatic temperament on which events make little impression.

Let it be perfectly clear that I claim no powers of prophetic hand analysis, and also that I do not believe such powers exist. It is true that I have on occasion made predictions about certain persons which have, with amazing accuracy, been realized. My explanation of this phenomenon is that, given complete understanding of all the factors in a situation, one can foresee a probability which is tantamount to almost certain prediction. Of course, in considering only the factors of a personality we do not allow for the action of outside circumstances which do not show in the hand until after they have made an impact on the personality. But we can judge with great accuracy what that impact will be on a person whom we completely understand.

When, therefore, I speak of danger of one kind or another threatening a person, I mean danger to which the weakness of that particular individual leaves him open. Such a danger may even be evaded through the use of more complete understanding gained from the study of the hand.

One of the most striking evidences supporting the claims of chirology to some share in the name of science is the fact that hands do change. No line or sign is at any time immutable. As the person to whom the hand belongs undergoes certain experiences, or changes his attitude, his ambitions, his thoughts; so do his hands register those changes.

COLOR

Now, as to the lines themselves. They should be well-marked and pinkish in color. A reddish line indicates an active, energetic and sanguinary disposition. Pale lines go with delicate health and

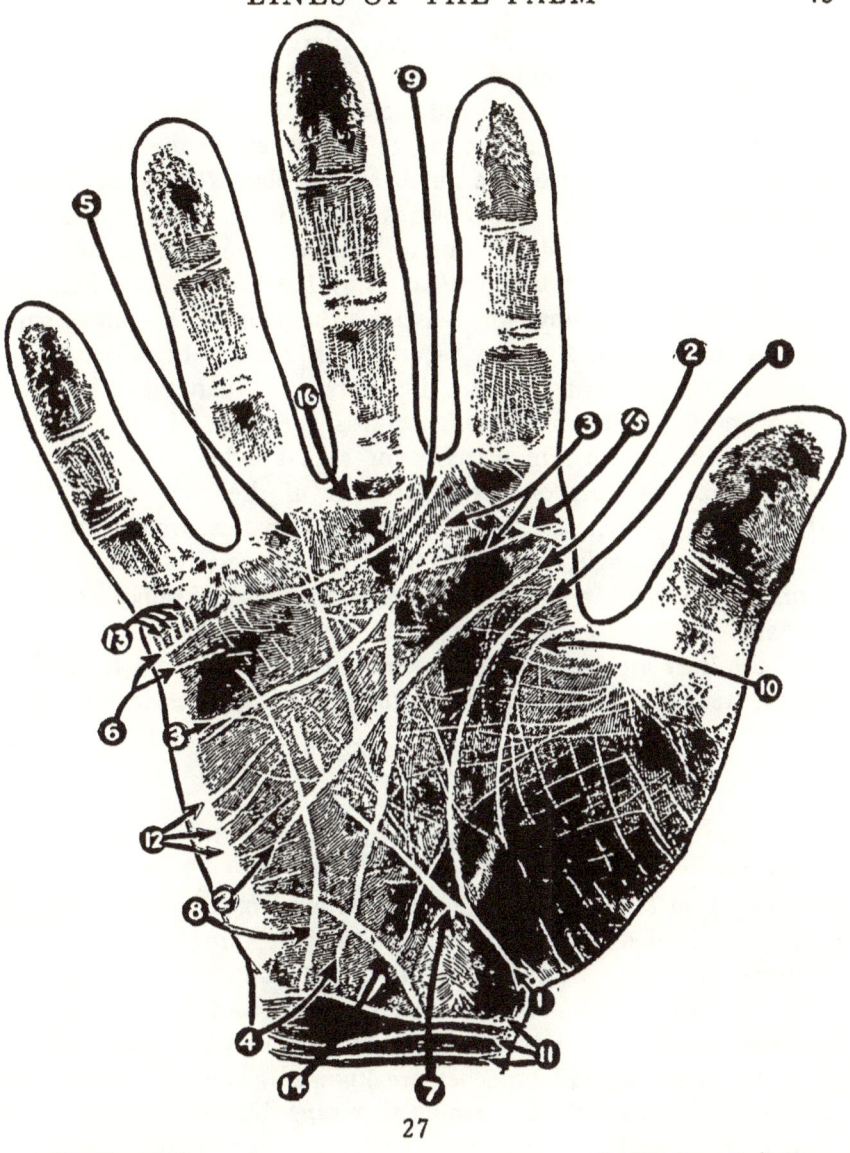

27

1. The line of life
2. The line of head
3. The line of heart
4. The line of destiny
5. The line of Apollo
6. The lines of sex
   influence

7. The lines of health or
   Hepatica
8. The lines of intuition
9. The girdle of Venus

10. The line of vitality
11. The bracelets
12. The lines of travel
13. The lines of fertility
14. The *via Lascivia*
15. The ring of Solomon
16. The ring of Saturn

lack of energy. Lines which are very dark show a melancholy, brooding temperament, vengeful and unforgiving.

The principal lines of the hand are shown in plate 27. They are seven in number: first, the line of life which bounds the mounts of Venus and Mars positive (see number 1 on plate 27); second, the line of head (number 2) which begins on the inner side of the palm and runs across it; third, the line of heart or emotions, pursuing a path across the hand above that taken by the line of head; fourth, the line of fate or destiny, which ascends the palm of the hand from the wrist towards the finger of Saturn; fifth, the line of sun or brilliance, which follows a path roughly parallel to that taken by the line of destiny, directing itself towards the base of the Apollo finger; sixth, the lines of marriage or sexual influence, which are short, horizontal lines on the outer edge of the palm under the little finger; and last, the line of health or Hepatica, which runs up the hand at an angle, ascending from the line of life toward the mount of Mercury. In addition, there are a number of minor lines in the hand.

All the lines are not always present in every hand, and their absence is frequently of even greater significance than is their presence.

QUALITY

The continuity of line is of great significance. Breaks (see plate 28 for examples of the formations cited in this and the following paragraph) in any line mean an obstruction, sometimes overcome, if they are healed by squares or supported by other strengthening influences. Unevenness in the line shows just that in the attribute— variability. Fine lines are often seen branching out from the main lines and usually show a weakening of the main pathway, indicating uncertainty. Such small branches are known as splits. If a split is directed towards a particular mount, it means that the subject is influenced by the attributes of that particular mount. The branching line often throws an interesting light on the main tendencies, telling about anything from a moment's diversion to a serious change in the direction of one's life.

Sister lines, that is lines running independently but parallel to a main line, add strength. But a sister line should not be confused with the island, which may run parallel to a main line for some distance, but is attached to it at either end, thus forming a sort of enclosure. An island very much weakens the main line at the point where it makes its appearance. Chained formations, dots, many

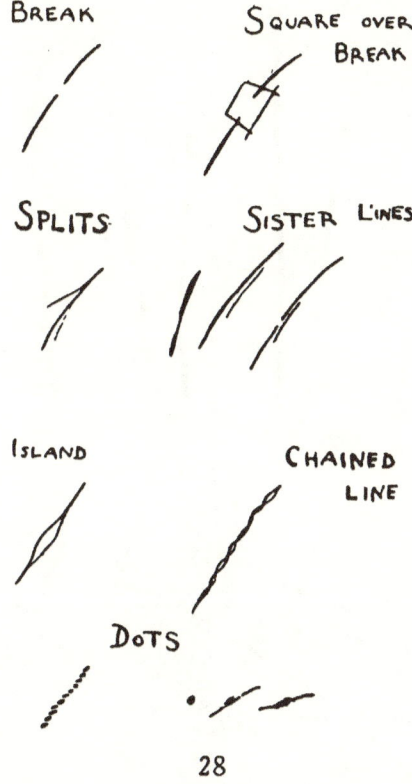

28

crossed lines—all react adversely on the primary line, and I shall discuss them in relation to the particular lines wherever they have special significance.

The best lines are clear, deep, without breaks or interfering markings of any kind. Very broad lines show more muscular strength than will power; while a deep, thin line holds up better under strain.

TIME AND AGE IN THE HAND

Using the main lines of the hand as guidemarks, we are able to compute time and age on the hand. Thus the approximate date associated with breaks, periods of restlessness and dissatisfaction, shifts

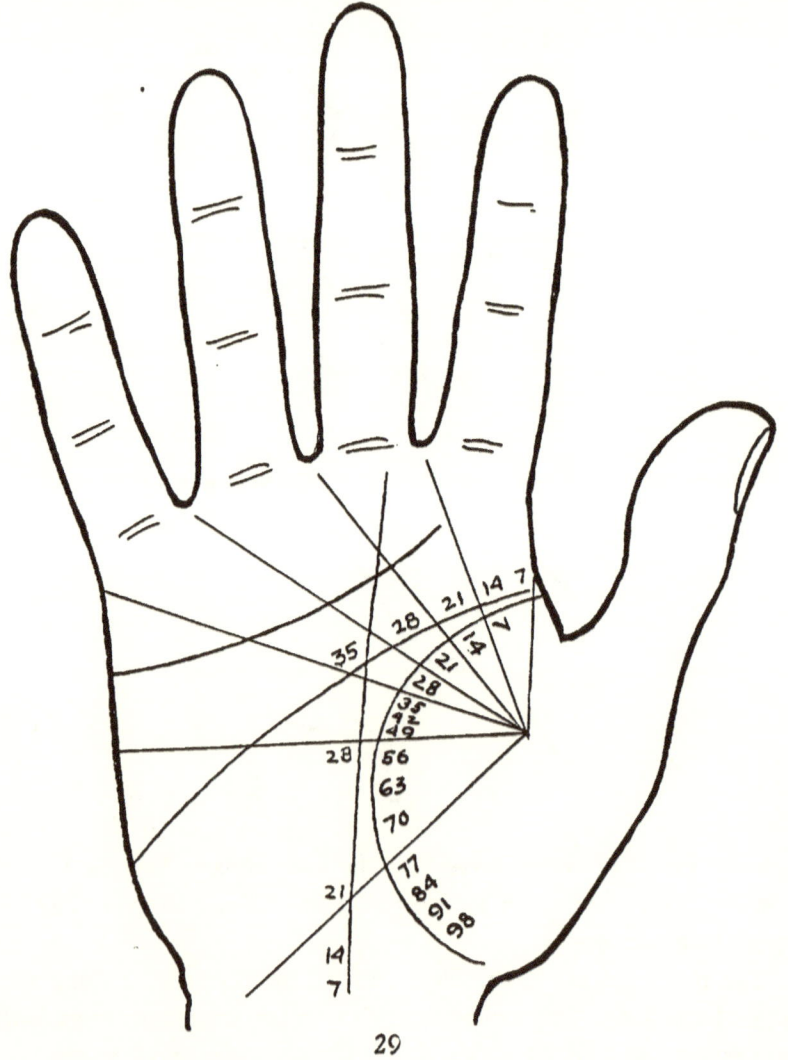

29

in occupation, can all be calculated from the hand. The only date which does not show is that which gives the subject's age.

The method of approximating dates in the hand is simple. Divide the maximum length possible for the line of life, the headline, the heartline and the line of destiny each into periods of seven as shown in plate 29. This is a very natural division since important physical changes in human beings are supposed to occur within cycles of seven years. Other markings on the hand can be related to this scheme by drawing radial lines from mount Venus through the seven divisions on the line of life and extending those imaginary radial lines to whatever event you wish to place in time. This, too, is shown in plate 29. To estimate the probable length of life, add the number of periods in these four principal lines of the hand—the lines of head, heart, destiny and life—and divide your total by four.

Of course, markings which are fixed in their place will have their own time scheme pertaining to them alone. For example, the marriage lines are figured within the confines of the space which they occupy, not in accordance with the plan of the whole hand, but this is explained in greater detail in my discussion of the marriage lines themselves.

Chapter VII.   THE LINE OF LIFE

THE line of life (see plate 27, number 1) bounds the mounts of Venus and Mars positive, fencing in the entire region about the base of the thumb. Its beginning is under the finger of Jupiter, its end in most cases under the mount of Venus, at the wrist. This line, according to the older theories of palmistry, was supposed to indicate longevity and the times when disease or danger threatened.

This I have found to be an extremely literal interpretation of the lifeline's actual function, which is to give an index of your health.

I have seen hands in which an actual break or even the ending of the line of life has not been followed by any dire results. Strong lines of the head and heart and a good thumb often overcome the indications of weakness in the line of life, and to conclude that a person's life is actually in danger at any given period, the hand analyst must look for confirmation in other parts of the hand. The clearest sign of departure from this life is the stopping of all the principal lines at the same date.

If the line of life is made up of little pieces, broken, or linked together, vitality is weak, often because of poor digestive functioning.

When the line of life commences high under the first finger the subject will be ambitious and well controlled, directing his energies to the attainment of his ambitions. A lower origin shows the opposite. The usual point at which the line of life begins is about halfway between the thumb and the base of the index finger.

The line of life may also vary in its termination. If it swerves toward the mount of Luna on the opposite side of the hand (see plate 30), it indicates a restless nature which may lead to wide travel

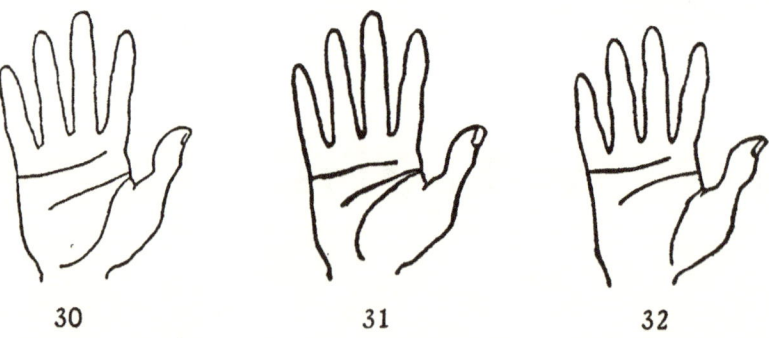

30   31   32

and residence and death in a foreign land. The sudden termination of the line of life, marked by a star or cross, shows the threat of sudden death or accident, especially if other signs in the hand bear out this warning.

If the line of life arcs far out into the hand (see plate 31), enlarging the space occupied by the mount of Venus, you will find a warm, generous and sympathetic nature; if Venus is constricted into a narrow space (see plate 32), you are likely to find a cold and selfish one.

Chapter VIII. THE LINE OF THE HEAD

THE line of head (see plate 27, number 2), showing mental balance, control, interests, depth, and concentration, is one of the most important lines of the hand. Its normal position lies in a course across the palm, about midway between the wrist and the base of the fingers. This line requires very careful study, for its most minute variations are of significance. Particularly should the two hands be compared as to their headlines; for early training, environment, and the effects of outside circumstances on the mental characteristics of a person often outweigh the influence of heredity. The right hand, of course, indicates our composite personality, the left, our natural endowments. If you are lefthanded, the reverse will be the case, for the left hand is then the operative one.

First, study the quality of the line. The best headline is clear, reddish in color and deep. With such a line, you can expect the ability to concentrate, sound judgment, a good memory, and vigorous, keen thought. A broad, shallow line indicates less precision and sureness, but, though the mind may be less penetrating, it is not necessarily less purposeful. It is the chained line (see plate 28) which shows flightiness and lack of concentration.

Often you will find a line which varies in quality through its length. In that case, the mental abilities will differ at various periods of life. Sometimes the cause of such variation will be apparent in other signs of the hand. The life line may, for example, show a serious illness at the time the line of head is of inferior quality, or the line of heart may indicate emotional unbalance for a period.

A broken line is always unfortunate. In the headline, a break shows impairment or interference with thinking and memory. When there are dots or islands at the termination of a break, the injury is the more serious. If the break is repaired by a square, or bridged by a sister line running parallel to the main line and close by it, the ill effects of whatever is responsible for the break may be largely discounted. Refer back to plate 28 for examples of these variations in a line.

The course of the line of head is often altered by small rises or deflections downwards. For example, it may arch upwards under the middle finger. In that case, the qualities associated with the mount of Saturn and the Saturn finger—seriousness, thoughtfulness, prudence in money matters—are a strong influence on the thought patterns. If the rise in the headline occurs towards the finger of Apollo, then the artistic sensibilities, lightness and gaiety of Apollo must be connected with the line's change in direction. As a rule, small dips in the line of head are considered signs of depression, rising arches, signs of good spirits or of an uplifting influence.

The most usual place of origin for the line of head coincides with the beginning of the line of life (see plate 33), the two lines being joined together for a short distance. This indicates caution, timidity

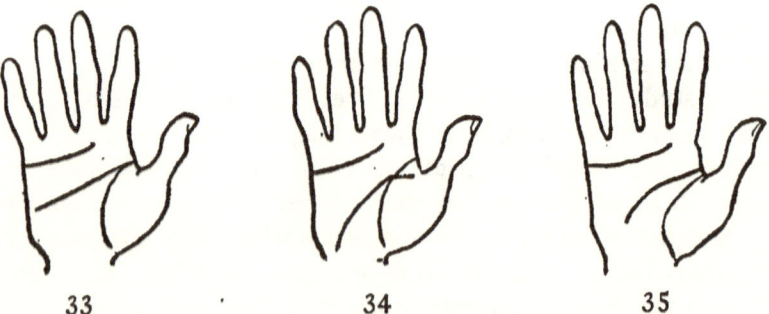

33 · 34 35

and dependence on others at the beginning of life. The earlier the two lines separate, the sooner will self-reliance be manifested.

When the line of head begins inside the line of life (see plate 34), the negative qualities associated with the first position are very much exaggerated. In a person with this formation, you find very little self-confidence. You will find nervous apprehensions inflated into phobias. You will see a person who is supersensitive, always looking for slights, lacking control. A person with a headline beginning in this position is very often a solitary individual, not necessarily by inclination, but because he is too timid to dare the criticism of his fellows and the give and take which social contacts entail.

A line of head beginning about midway between the origin of the line of life and the base of the first finger (see plate 35) is a strong indication of well-balanced, independent headwork. Such a line shows self-confidence without conceit, an energetic, daring mind, not bound to pathways followed by conventional thinkers. With such a headline, there is usually strong ambition and the mental clarity needed to realize that ambition. Of course, the quality of the line itself will modify the indications of its position, but, on the whole, a headline with this origin is strong augury of success.

When the space between the line of life and the headline is widened, and the latter begins high up on the side of the hand near the base of the first finger (see plate 36), the quality of self-reliance is turned to recklessness. A person with his headline beginning so close to the finger of Jupiter is too conceited to listen to the counsel of others, too impatient to base his actions on careful judgment. He is a gambler, thoughtless of consequences, careless of his actions' effect on others. When this high headline is short, a jealous temperament is also shown.

Usually the line of head commences at the edge of the hand. One exception to this position is found in the line which leaves a slight margin at the side and commences under the finger of Jupiter (see plate 37). Strong ambition will motivate the thinking of a person with this kind of headline. Usually a headline having this origin is good in quality, and there is every probability of fulfilling the ambition unless a weak thumb and generally forceless hand gainsay its promise.

The course followed by the line of head and its termination must be read in conjunction with the origin. A straight, even path (see plate 33) denotes good mental balance, excellent control, and a mind which is neither too taken up with fantasy nor too restricted by small, practical considerations. A straight course will do much to counteract the weakness implied by an origin coinciding with the line of life and will to some extent reduce the timidity and oversensitiveness of a headline which begins inside the space enclosed by the line of life. With a headline which starts outside the line of life,

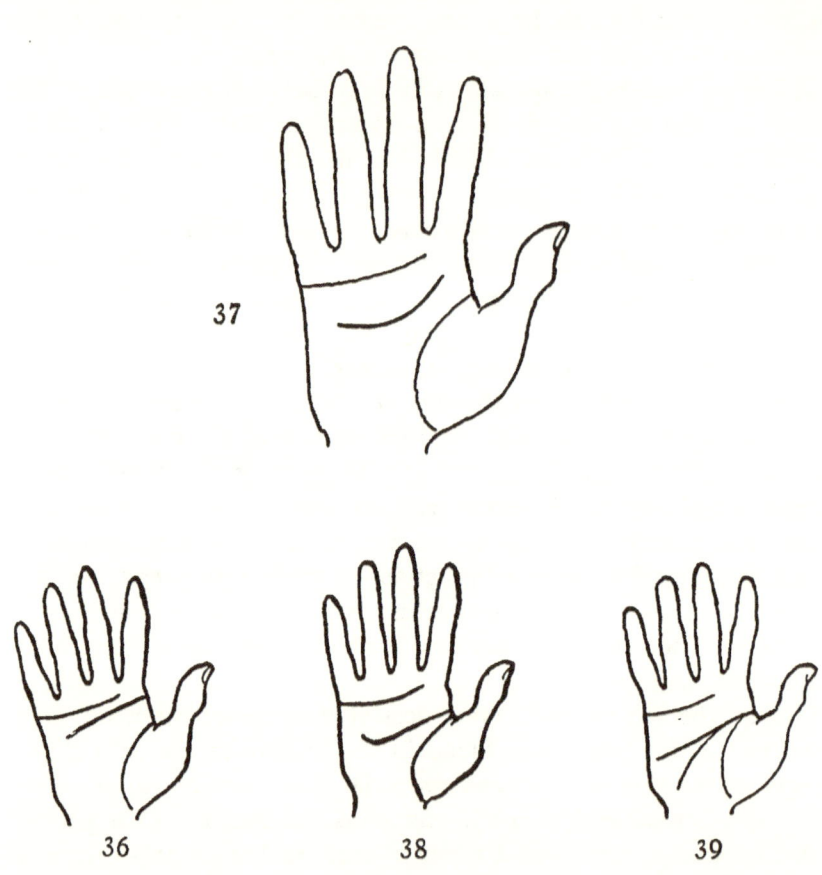

a straight, even course is a brilliant indication. Its balance will even somewhat counteract the recklessness of a line starting too high on the hand.

When the line of head points in a downward direction or ends in a sharp curve towards the mount of Luna (see plates 34 and 35), the faculties of imagination and fantasy, represented by that mount, will govern the mind. In a weak hand, one lacking will and force, one in which the origin of the line of head shows excessive timidity, this direction is unpromising. It gives us the dreamer, the introspective builder of castles in the air, the conqueror of non-existent empires. But, when there is sufficient strength to use the gift of creative imagination, a headline dipping onto Luna is the mark of the artist, the writer, the discoverer, the man or woman who is not afraid to venture beyond the realms of known fact. The best combination with a headline descending onto Luna is one which begins outside the line of life, but not too high on the side of the hand (see plate 35). The worst is a headline commencing inside the line of life (see plate 34), for with so little mental balance and self-confidence, there is always danger that a strongly imaginative person will take refuge completely in his land of make-believe, becoming the victim of delusions and fancies. A star at the termination of a headline of this character is even stronger indication of insanity, especially when the quality of the line is also poor—chained or much broken up.

A headline which curves up towards Mercury (see plate 37) shows a practical mind, taken up with the problems of business and material existence. On a narrow hand this line will indicate an excessively humdrum man of affairs, concerned with nothing but material success, very positive and bigoted in his opinions. On a broad, active hand, it still does not show great liberality of mind, but at least it does not reveal a narrow-minded fanatic. It will indicate a person who looks at material things in a broader perspective, though one who is impatient of things which are not of immediate utility.

When there is a sort of double curve in the line of head, first down and then up, like the letter "S" (see plate 38), you have a person with complete coordination of the mental and muscular processes, in other words, an athlete. I found this double curve in the headlines of persons as diverse in their general makeup as William Tilden, Babe Ruth, Spencer Tracy, Gene Tunney, Jack Dempsey and Helen Wills Moody. One thing they all have in common—the wonderful control of their muscular reactions which made them champion athletes.

A forked headline (see plate 39), one ending in two or more branches, may mean one of two things, depending on the strength of the hand. In a strong hand, the added branch gives versatility. For example, a straight headline with a branch descending onto the mount of Luna will show the soundly balanced judgment and clear reasoning power of the straight line plus imagination. In a weak hand, such a forking results in uncertainty and vacillation.

The general position of the line of head is also of significance. If the line is very high, thus overshadowing the line of heart, you have a strongly rational being whose emotions are completely controlled by his mind. When, on the other hand, the line of heart is placed low, close to the line of head, mental balance will be more precarious, subject to the vagaries of the emotions.

Chapter IX. THE LINE OF HEART

THE line of heart (see plate 27, number 3), running across the palm above the line of head, shows emotional steadfastness and intensity. This line must be read in conjunction with the indications of the hand as a whole and particularly in relation to the line of head.

The quality of the heartline is of course significant. As with all the other lines of the hand, its best formation is a clear, deep drawing, neither too broad nor too narrow, and of good color. A line which is uniformly of this character, throughout its entire length, will show strong, consistent affections, loyalty, sympathy and balance.

If the heartline is thin, your subject will be self-centered and cold. This lack of feeling is likely to be combined with a narrow-minded, conventional attitude. The line must, however, be thin in relation to the other lines of the hand to make this interpretation a correct one.

A broad, shallow line of heart discloses affections easily given and as easily withdrawn—inconsistency, changeableness. Fickleness of a different sort is indicated by a deeply chained line of heart. With such, there may be great intensity but still no reliability. The person with a deep, chained line of heart meets this one-and-only love every other day, feels the world reborn and then dying through the course of each affair, and is immediately off to the next.

Lines cutting across the line of heart tell of worries and obstacles in the course of true love. In its path across the hand, the line of heart may give off many small branches or splits. Splits rising from the heart line towards any one of the mounts show the attraction of the mount's characteristics over the affections of the subject. For example, a person with many little hairlines rising from the line of heart toward the mount of Apollo will be much attracted by someone in whom the artistic sensibility and gaiety of the Apollonian predominate. Lines falling from the line of heart towards the line of head show conflict between judgment and the emotions, often also disappointments in love.

Of course, in studying the character of the line of heart, we must look at it in segments. The line frequently changes its nature a number of times during its course across the hand. In such case, the emotional vagaries associated with a particular type of line apply only to the period of life spanned by that section of the line. A naturally affectionate person may, because of uncongenial surroundings, become extremely self-contained and apparently cold, only to flower out into sympathetic warmth on receiving understanding.

As with the line of head, the origin of the heartline is of great significance. The line of heart may start anywhere from the very edge of the palm to a position more than halfway across the hand. If it begins far out at the edge (see plate 40), you have an emotional extremist, blindly enthusiastic in love, submerging every other ambition and desire in his intense emotionalism, losing all reason and balance. The nature of the line will show whether a person is given to periodic emotional extravagances or combines constancy with intensity. In either case, his emotional abandon is likely to bring grief, for he follows the dictates of his feelings without regard to the cautionings of his mind.

A line of heart beginning under the finger of Jupiter (see plate 41) still gives us the idealist in love, one who sentimentalizes both his affections and the object of them, but this position does allow a measure of control. With this heartline, constancy is likely to be an outstanding trait, for its bearer is almost as well satisfied with the shadow of romance as with the actuality and will console himself with an ideal if the reality fades. A forked beginning on Jupiter increases the sentimentality.

When the line of heart originates betwen the first and second fingers (see plate 42), we have the realist in love who combines

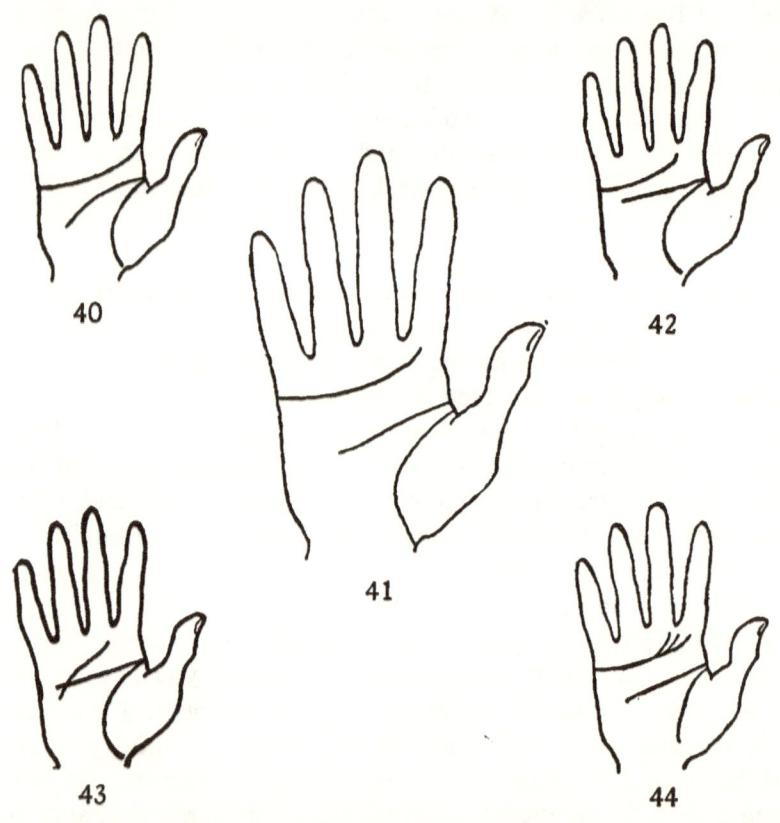

practicality with his affections. Such a person is likely to be cautious in his choice of those he loves, but warmly devoted after he has come to a decision. He will coordinate ambition with love and will be strongly held by family ties.

A line of heart rising from the mount of Saturn (see plate 43) indicates the sensualist, a person whose love is more passionate than sentimental or affectionate. This will be particularly true if the mount of Venus is well developed at its base and pink or red in color.

When the line of heart begins in a three-pronged fork, one branch under Jupiter, one under Saturn and the middle branch between the two fingers (see plate 44), it shows a balanced union of idealism, practicality and passion and usually indicates that the heart is the dominant factor in the personality. With this forked origin on the heartline, a strong line of head and a well-developed thumb are needed to keep the individual from being submerged in his emotions.

The line of heart varies in its termination as well as in its beginning. Should it cross the hand completely, from one side to the other (see plate 40), the strength of the emotions is increased, giving us a person who is buffeted and torn by his feelings. Such a person will be jealous and possessive, especially if the plain of Mars shows excessive development.

A termination of the line of heart directed upwards towards any of the mounts shows unusually strong influence and attraction from persons having the attributes of those mounts. A downward bend at the end of the line of heart gives the affections dominion over reason. When the heart line actually cuts through the line of head (see plate 43), you may look for serious mental disturbance as a result of emotional instability.

Sometimes you find only one line in a hand instead of two separate lines, one governing the head and one the heart. Even when this line is placed high in the hand, in the normal position for the line of heart, it must be considered as the line of head, not of heart. I have encountered this formation only rarely and always in the hands of men who had an unchangeable intensity of purpose, an overwhelming, directed ambition. Sir Basil Zaharoff, the munitions king and merchant of death, had this single combined head-and-heart line, and so had Andrew Mellon, the American financier.

Chapter X. THE LINE OF DESTINY

THE line of destiny or Saturn (see plate 27, number 4), tells the plan of life, and whether that plan will be easily fulfilled or meet with many obstacles. When the destiny line is deep, clear and without interfering cross markings, you may expect a career pursued with determination and leading to success. It is true that I have occasionally found hands in which this line was entirely lacking, but such instances are rare. When there was no line of destiny, I have found my subject one who has made his own way in life, entirely unassisted by friends, influence or luck, except as those aids were brought into play through the man's own ingenuity.

The strength of a happy augury is much diminished if the Saturn line is very broad, pale and shallow, much more so than the other markings in the hand. In that case, you may be sure that natural talents were wasted and energy applied much too haphazardly to realize the hand's full promise. When the line is very thin and light, it indicates a lack of forcefulness which interferes with success.

Breaks in the line of destiny show some obstacle in the career sufficiently strong to interrupt it. If the break is healed over by a square, or carried by a sister line paralleling the broken line of destiny, the interruption will be less serious, the obstacle overcome. Sometimes, the line of destiny takes up an entirely new course after a break, showing that the interference has directed you into new endeavors. Whether the change is to your benefit is shown by the quality of the line, both before and after the break. Should the line be stronger and clearer when it resumes its course, your new career will be more promising than the abandoned one.

Frequently, I find the line of destiny cut by either the line of head or the line of heart, sometimes both, with marked breaks occurring at the crossing. When the interference comes from the line of head, you may be sure that some mistake in judgment has caused your life's work to be interrupted. If the line of head actually stops the Saturn line in its ascent (see plate 45), poor judgment has indeed seriously blocked your chances of success. Such ill omens are, however, not permanent unless you allow yourself to be discouraged by them. I have observed fate lines, thus stopped, begin a new

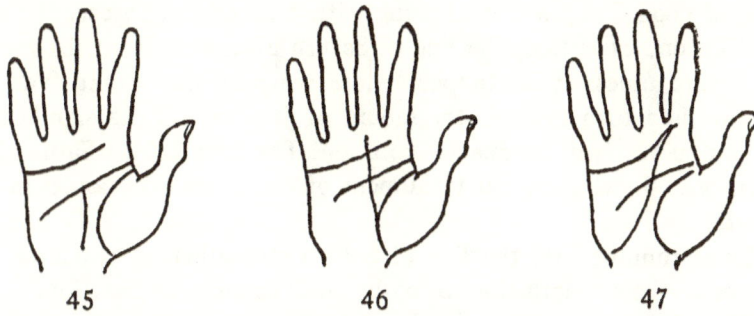

45   46   47

growth as courage returned and the person tried to build another career. Sometimes, the new line is of much better quality than the one which ended so ominously.

Interference with the line of Saturn from the line of heart shows emotional unbalance to be the cause of an upset. Here again, as in the case of hindrance from the line of head, the seriousness of the break must be judged both from the indications of healing which are present, such as a square or a parallel line, as well as from the course and strength of the line of Saturn after the break.

The space between the lines of head and heart is frequently the least promising portion of the line of destiny. This period corresponds with the ages from about 30 to 45 years, often the most active of one's life. Whether or not you are able to overcome the vicissitudes and demands of this time of life is shown by the terminal of the Saturn line. If it resumes its course stronger than ever after having passed the line of heart, the middle years will serve to enrich your life and make success taste the sweeter. If the line of Saturn becomes wavery, thin and broken at its end, then the difficulties of this period will have proved too much. Again, however, I want to remind you that the black and white differences which the old superstition of palmistry assigned to such marks cannot be accepted blindly. I have found hands which indicated extreme misfortune completely changed as their owners understood their difficulties and overcame them.

All lines cutting across the line of Saturn weaken it, and their place of origin will usually explain their nature. Lines rising from the mount of Luna indicate that impractical, fantastic imagination is proving an obstacle; lines from the mount of Venus, that sloth and love of good living are interfering with a successful career.

With one exception, the line of Saturn always ends on the mount of Saturn unless it is stopped before reaching that point. The exception is a turn towards the mount of Jupiter, and its significance is that success will be due to ambition. The terminal on Saturn is a good one, showing logical fulfillment of the talents contained in the hand.

Lines running into the line of Saturn strengthen it, revealing the source of the strength they bring by their origin and direction.

Though the line of Saturn does not vary much in its termination, it may begin from a number of places. Its most usual origin is from the center of the palm near the wrist. This origin is the normal one, showing that a person has taken his direction fairly early in life. When the line of destiny begins from the line of life (see plate 46), a person's own efforts are largely responsible for whatever success he attains, and the higher on the line of life the beginning of the Saturn line, the later will success be achieved.

The opposite is shown by a line of destiny originating on the mount of Luna (see plate 47). This shows the aid and influence of friends, relatives and family connections. If the line of destiny, beginning on the mount of Luna, later merges into the line of heart (see plate 47), this aid is likely due to a brilliant and most fortunate marriage, combining an ideal relationship with wealth and ease.

A line of destiny beginning at the wrist and making its way straight and unbroken to the base of mount Saturn, without branches or influences of any kind along its entire length, marks a person out as a plaything of fate, tossed about by forces more powerful than he. With a star at both the origin and termination of a fate line of this character, you can also expect some awful, twisted kind of fame or notoriety.

Chapter XI.   THE LINE OF APOLLO

THOUGH the line of Apollo (see plate 27, number 5) is accounted one of the major lines of the hand, it is not present in every hand, nor even in the majority. Yet, without it, the hand is a poor thing, promising hardship and struggle without assurance of success. The line of Apollo, which runs from the wrist towards the base of the third finger, is the line of luck or fortune. In many hands, this line is missing until quite late in life. After it puts in its appearance, the entire life becomes changed, assuming a more optimistic, easy aspect.

Both the length of this line and its quality determine to what extent its force is operative. Defects in its structure greatly reduce its influence. Islands, for example, practically nullify its effect for the period represented by the malformation. Dots, to the extent that any sign can be so definitely associated with a single meaning, I have found connected with loss of reputation and notoriety. Breaks in the line show difficulties or interruptions to good fortune; cross bars, contrary influences.

As to the line itself, the longer it is, the longer will good fortune last. Sometimes the line of Apollo acts as a sister line for that of Saturn, becoming stronger when the latter dims and itself fading when the line of Saturn gains strength.

The line of Apollo always runs in the direction of the Apollo finger, though it may stop short of that goal. A firm line, clean and deep at its termination means success crowning the termination of your life. If the line loses strength or ends before reaching the mount of Apollo, the end of life will contain some disappointments, not necessarily reverses in business, loss of fortune or a bad outcome to your career, but possibly disappointments connected with your family, children, or others on whom your own happiness depends. Fading of the Apollo line towards its end may also show a change of disposition to a more sombre hue, such as is characteristic of certain illnesses which afflict old age.

If there is a sign at the end of the line, this must be considered in conjunction with the line. A dot, as in other portions of the line, shows loss of reputation. A deep bar cutting off the line indicates an insurmountable obstacle near the close of the life. Should the life line exhibit weakness at the age of about fifty, then such a bar is likely to be an illness or delicate health. A cross marking the termination of the line of Apollo is often a sign of foolhardiness causing ill repute, and the line of head should be looked at carefully to see whether it bears out this indication of poor judgment. An island at the end of the Apollo line negatives much of the line's efficacy, telling that life is likely to close under some sort of shadow, usually associated with loss of wealth and reputation.

These are the unfortunate signs on the line of Apollo. The more desirable ones are a square, a trident (see plate 48) and, above all, a star. With a star at the termination of the Apollo line, you have strong assurance of brilliant success. I have found this sign in the hands of financiers, writers, artists and statesmen, and in every case, these persons have felt themselves blessed by some kind of lucky fortune, something for which they themselves could not account, but which seemed to direct all their undertakings to fortunate conclusions. The square is, as always, a healing mark, operating against all the defects of the line throughout its entire length.

A forked ending is not altogether favorable. It shows a diversity of talents which may, if concentration and determination are lacking, lead to dissipation of your endowments. But when the fork assumes the shape of a well-marked trident, this is almost as fortunate as a star because it indicates wealth and celebrity achieved through mental efforts. The star is less specific in its promise, but is frequently associated in some way with the arts or the theater.

The Apollo line may, near its end, branch off to mount Saturn or Mercury. In such case, add the wisdom of Saturn or the shrewdness

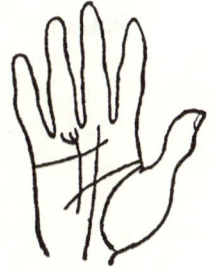

48

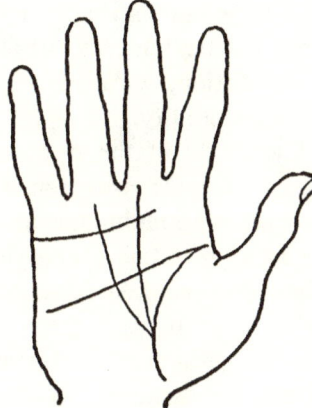

49

50

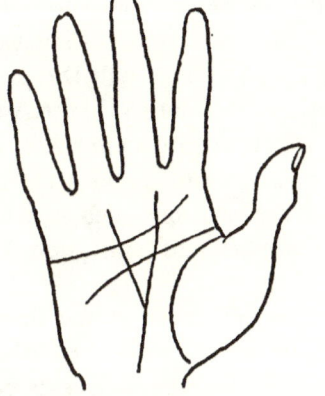

51

and business judgment of Mercury to the brilliance of Apollo. Other branches from the line can be regarded much in the same light. When they take a rising direction, they are favorable, and their specific application can be deduced from the direction in which they point. Falling branches and hairlines show the need for greater concentration and effort to enjoy the full benefit of a good Apollo line.

Now as to the nature of the line itself. Of course, a sharp, deep, clearcut line with good color is best. A broad, shallow line gives a rather surface appreciation of the arts and some success in connection with them, but it also carries the implication of great show and a false front. A chained line, especially when it is shallow, gives the hollow semblance of success and reputation—one who talks much about his attainments but fools no one but himself. A wavy line tells of vacillation, a career which suffers because of erratic waverings and unreliability.

The origin of the Apollo line modifies its significance to a slight degree. When it rises from the mount of Luna (see plate 49), it will show strong imagination joined to good powers of expression. Such a line is a great boon for writers, lecturers and speakers of all kinds. When the line of Apollo starts from the wrist and runs all the way to the Apollo mount, it has its greatest length and will throw its fortunate influence over the entire life. If the line starts low, but runs only for a short distance, unusual talents and opportunities of early life will be frittered away.

The line of Apollo beginning from the line of life (see plate 50), is usually associated with success in artistic work, the higher its point of origin on the lifeline, the later will the career bear fruit. Starting from the line of destiny (see plate 51), the Apollo line places a crown of good fortune on a person's own efforts. A beginning from the line of head adds luck to brain work, and a start from the line of heart indicates very happy sex relations such as a marriage which will contribute to happiness, wealth and reputation. Usually, this last indication applies to the latter part of life.

To some extent, the influences of the lines of Apollo and Saturn are overlapping. They can, however, be distinguished in this way. The Saturn line refers more to the active career. The Apollo line governs the chance and luck attending that career. Apollo applies particularly to the outward semblances of success—wealth and reputation.

As to the way in which this line makes its influence apparent, that I have not been able to explain to my entire satisfaction. Many other signs in the hand which had previously been assigned a superstitious rather than a psychological or physiological significance, I have been able to consider in a more scientific light. At first, I was inclined to discount the influence of the Apollo line entirely, but actual study of many thousands of hands taught me that persons who lacked this line were practically always beset by difficulties, no matter how favorable the other indications in their hands. On the other hand, those who possessed this sign of fortune seemed favored by luck, chance—call it what you will. Whether there is some mysterious element in the chemistry of personality which determines probabilities of fortune with mathematical precision, I would not dare say. But even this indication will some day, I venture to guess, be fully explained in terms which allow no doubt.

Chapter XII. THE LINES OF SEX INFLUENCE

ON the outer edge of the hand, extending into the palm under the little finger, there are often a number of horizontal lines. These are the lines of sex influence (see plate 27, number 6), or, as the older followers of palmistry termed them, the lines of marriage. They do not, of course, show the number of times you have married or will marry. What they do show is the number, depth and constancy of the sexual attractions which your personality complex makes possible for you. Some of these relations may be realized, possibly in friendship with the opposite sex in which attraction plays a large part, possibly in marriage, whether actually legalized or not. For, of course, a deeply felt and stable sexual relation will show on the hand regardless of the seal of civil and spiritual authority.

When the marriage lines—I shall use the older term because of its greater facility—are close to the line of heart (see the lowest of the three short lines in plate 52), they apply to youth. In the middle of the space between the line of heart and the base of the finger of

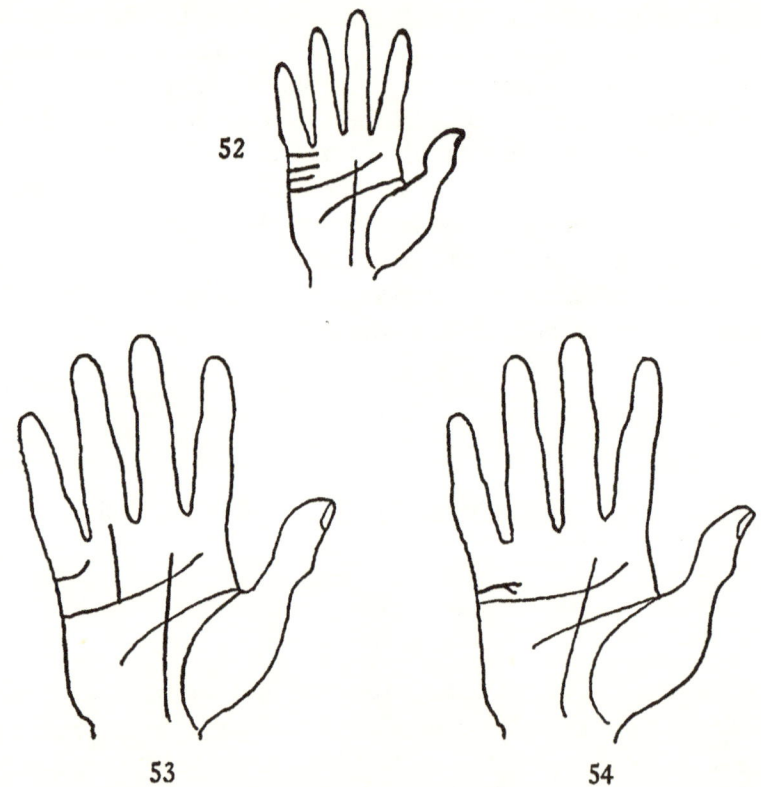

Mercury, marriage lines are placed at the ages of about twenty-five and thirty. The closer to the finger of Mercury they appear (see the uppermost of the three short lines in plate 52), the greater the age to which they refer.

A marriage line which turns up toward the finger of Mercury (see plate 53) is usually found without companion lines and shows a person who is "not the marrying kind." A look at the line of heart will often disclose the reason—whether it be fickleness as indicated by a broad, chained line of heart or the bleak, self-centered disposition which goes with a thin, bare line of heart.

A fork at the end of the marriage line, especially one curving down into the hand (see plate 54), indicates the probability of separation or divorce, and a downward curve alone has the same significance.

The longer and clearer the line of sex influence, the more stable and deep will be the relationship. One of the strongest indications of a happy marriage is an influence line from the mount of Luna into the line of destiny, combined with a single, long and clearly marked line of marriage. A wealthy marriage is sometimes thought to be shown by a marriage line merging into the line of Apollo.

If the line of marriage is broken up or linked like a chain, the relationship will be very unhappy. The cause of such unhappiness— physiological differences, diversity in interests or in temperament— might be discovered by a comparison of the hands of two people contemplating a union.

LINES OF FERTILITY

The small, vertical lines which stand up between the lines of marriage on the side of the hand (see plate 27, number 13) indicate fertility—the number of children you *can* have, not at all necessarily the number you *will* have. Usually, they are much more clearly marked in the hands of women than of men. Broad and deep lines are taken by the lore of palmistry to indicate male children; narrow, fine lines, females. Very faint and uneven lines show delicacy in the offspring. Straight, deep, clear ones indicate strong and healthy children. When one line of a group is markedly longer and stronger than the others, it shows the superiority of one of the children over his brothers and sisters.

A very flat mount of Venus and a bracelet which rises from the wrist into the palm of the hand is usually considered a sign of sterility.

Chapter XIII. THE LINE OF HEALTH OR HEPATICA

THE line of health or Hepatica (see plate 27, number 7), which runs down the hand in a diagonal direction, normally from the mount of Mercury toward the line of life, is classed among the major lines. It is, however, often absent altogether or only very faintly or fragmentarily present. Its total absence is the best indication of all, for this shows an extremely robust, resistant and energetic constitution.

Next to complete absence, a straight line, extending down the outer side of the palm from Mercury through the mount of Luna is a good second-best. Though this position does not indicate the complete escape from ills which absence shows, it still manifests great resistance to whatever ailments are contracted.

The point at which the line of health actually encounters the line of life, when the former takes its normal position in diagonal line, is one at which the health and life are seriously menaced. If the line of life is weak at this point, and if there is corroborating evidence in the lines of heart and head, this point can almost certainly be taken as the end of life.

Chapter XIV. THE MINOR LINES OF THE HAND

IN addition to the major lines, which are present in almost every hand, there are a number of minor groovings which your hand may or may not show. Some of these give valuable assistance to the talents and characteristics revealed by the rest of your hand. Others are less propitious.

THE LINE OF INTUITION

The line of intuition (see plate 27, number 8) is a mixed blessing. Its position is along the outer edge of the palm, running vertically from the Lunar mount to the mount of Mercury. Its shape is an arc, approaching the semi-circle, arching out into the palm.

The line of intuition, as its name indicates, gives its possessor acute, intuitive understanding. It marks out a sort of sixth sense by which things not perceived through the ordinary sensory faculties and not reasoned by the mind are seemingly arrived at by instinct. A deep, clear, unbroken line having a good arc will give the most reliable intuitive sensitiveness. A broken or otherwise defective line has little effectiveness, or it may show a false intuition. An island on the line likewise indicates intuitions either misapplied or only partially understood.

A branch line running from a deep, clear line of intuition to the Jupiter mount shows the realization of this mysterious faculty and its application to aid ambition. A rising line to the mount of Apollo shows a measure of renown coming from the use of this strange gift. Conflict is told by a line from this mark which cuts through the line of destiny. This indicates that the intuitive faculties will seriously prejudice the career. When the connecting line from the arc of intuition actually merges into the line of destiny, instinct will prove an aid to the career.

At times this line of intuition may be very broken up and confused with a defective line of health. In that case, the exercise of the intuitive faculties is a danger to health. For corroboration, look at the line of head. If it, too, shows weakness, there is danger that the attraction of mysticism will unbalance the mind.

Persons who possess this sixth sense are often unaware of it themselves. In any case, they are unable to explain it. To what extent it is connected with suggestibility and the manifestations of hypnosis, I do not know. Perhaps the faculty is a natural one which we have lost, corresponding to the racial memory and instincts of animals.

Perhaps it is a new sensory endowment which mankind is just in process of developing. That is the theory adopted by such scientists as Sir Oliver Lodge, who believe that some day all human beings will be able to receive impressions which are in no sense mysterious but merely too delicate to be registered by the fingers, eyes, ears and nose. If there do exist waves or particles which, functioning outside ordinary time, would tell us of the past or future, we may some day learn of them, just as we have found light waves which the eye does not register but which make their impression on sensitive instruments.

THE VIA LASCIVIA

The *via lascivia* (see plate 27, number 14) is a rare marking. It is a convex arch either crossing the hand above the wrist or slanting from lower mount Luna into the wrist. This line indicates great physical energy. If the hand as a whole is coarse and sensual, the *via lascivia* increases the sensuality, gluttony and passion shown by the hand. When the hand is a more ideal or mental type, the excess energy may be directed into work.

THE GIRDLE OF VENUS

The girdle of Venus (see plate 27, number 9) is an arc looping down into the palm from between the first and second fingers and the third and fourth. Occasionally, it stretches out from the Jupiter finger to the base of Mercury or even to the outer edge of the palm. It is in part a sister line to the line of heart and sometimes, when the later is absent, it takes its place.

Depending on the type of hand, the girdle of Venus has widely differing implications. On a sensitive hand, it is likely to mean nervous disorders, often connected with sex maladjustments. Many fine lines etched all over the palm will bear out the interpretation of nervous sensitiveness. When the headline is poor, the girdle of Venus may be taken as a symptom of hysteria.

In a hand which is strongly physical, the girdle of Venus emphasizes sensuality, sometimes, if it is both strong and much broken up, showing sexual abnormalities.

The further the girdle of Venus extends across the hand, the better, for proximity to the palms outer edge allows the stabilizing force of Mercury to be felt. When, in cutting through the lines of Saturn or Apollo, the girdle of Venus actually breaks them, sensuality or pre-occupation with sex will be an obstacle to success.

THE LINE OF VITALITY

The line of Mars or vitality (see plate 27, number 10) is a sister line to the line of life, running parallel to it and inside its enclosure. This line greatly strengthens a weak line of life and adds tremendous energy to a good one. Its aid is limited to the period during which it extends, and only when the line of vitality continues for the whole length of the line of life is its effect felt from birth to death. On the whole, the line of Mars is an excellent indication, but there is always the danger that the bounding energy and vitality it gives will lead to excesses of various kinds.

THE RING OF SOLOMON

The ring of Solomon (see plate 27, number 15) is a very unusual formation, made by an extension of the line of heart which, instead of rising on the mount of Jupiter, begins as a semicircle curling like a ring around the base of the Jupiter finger. This sign I have found associated with a very fastidious, sensitive nature, often possessing psychic or clairvoyant powers. Its presence, though at best rare, is more frequent in the hands of women than of men.

THE RING OF SATURN

The ring of Saturn (see plate 27, number 16) may be a line circling the base of the middle finger or formed of two lines starting on either side of that finger and crossing below it. It is an unfavorable sign, indicating lack of constancy and should be read as a warning to overcome vacillation and changeableness. To negate the effect of the ring of Saturn, a strong-willed thumb and good line of head should be present.

THE BRACELETS

The bracelets (see plate 27, number 11) are the rings on the wrist, defining the lower edge of the palm. They may be absent altogether or there may be one or two or, at the most, three. These used to be considered indications of longevity, a term of thirty years being arbitrarily assigned to each bracelet. In my studies of hands, I have found the bracelets to mean very little, except that the upcurving of the topmost one into the palm itself is strong indication of sterility.

THE LINES OF TRAVEL

The lines of travel (see plate 27, number 12) are actually not prophetic marks of future wanderings over the face of the earth, but rather the indications of a restlessness which may very well find its expression in voyagings. These lines are found cutting into the palm from far on the outer edge of the Lunar mount. They run in a diagonally upward direction. When the travel lines merge with the line of destiny, travel is likely to be your career or a part of it. As to fixing the date of the voyages, the diagram fixing time in the hand applies to these lines as to the others. Restlessness, the desire to be on the move, to see new places, people and things is stronger at some periods of life than others. Some persons are hit by wanderlust in their youth, others not until after they have satisfied other ambitions. That is the extent to which these lines fix the dates of voyages.

Chapter *XV.* SPECIAL MARKINGS IN THE PALM

IN addition to the eminences on the palm and the lines which cross it in all directions, you will often notice special formations. Each of these has its particular significance, modified by the position in which it is placed.

THE STAR

The star (see plate 55) is, with only two exceptions, one of the most fortunate signs to have. One negative implication is connected with a star on the line of head, particularly at its end (see plate 56, 1), which may be a sign of genius, but of that peculiar genius which crosses the border from sanity to insanity. A star on mount Saturn, under the middle finger, is the second unfortunate placement. This is manifestation of a dreaded kind of distinction, of notoriety and infamy more as the result of circumstances than through any wrong-doing of the person himself.

The more favorable placements of the star give great distinction. A star on the mount of Apollo (see plate 56, 3) is a sign of the greatest good luck, promising wealth, renown and happiness. This position is usually associated with a public career. A star on the positive mount of Mars above the Venus mount (see plate 56, 8), is more particularized, being usually associated with distinction in military affairs. On mount Jupiter (see plate 56, 12), a star signifies capacity for leadership and its realization. On mount Mercury (see plate 56, 4), the star promises success in the fields associated with that mount, science or commerce, according to the other indications of the hand. A star on the negative mount of Mars on the outer edge of the palm between the Lunar mount and that of Mercury (see plate 56, 7) promises recompense and honor for great moral courage. A star on mount Luna (see plate 56, 10) gives celebrity achieved through application of a vivid imagination. A star on mount Venus (see plate 56, 9) tells of unusual magnetism for the opposite sex. A star on the

STARS

CIRCLES

ISLANDS

TRIPODS

CROSSES

SQUARES

TRIANGLES

GRILLES

55

plain of Mars (see plate 56, 6) marks you for success in invention. Between the origin of the line of life and the line of destiny (see plate 56, 5), a star indicates prominence in theology. On the tip of the little finger (see plate 56, 11), a star emphasizes the facility with language which is associated with that finger and tells of spellbinding eloquence. On the tips of the other fingers (see plate 56, 13), stars

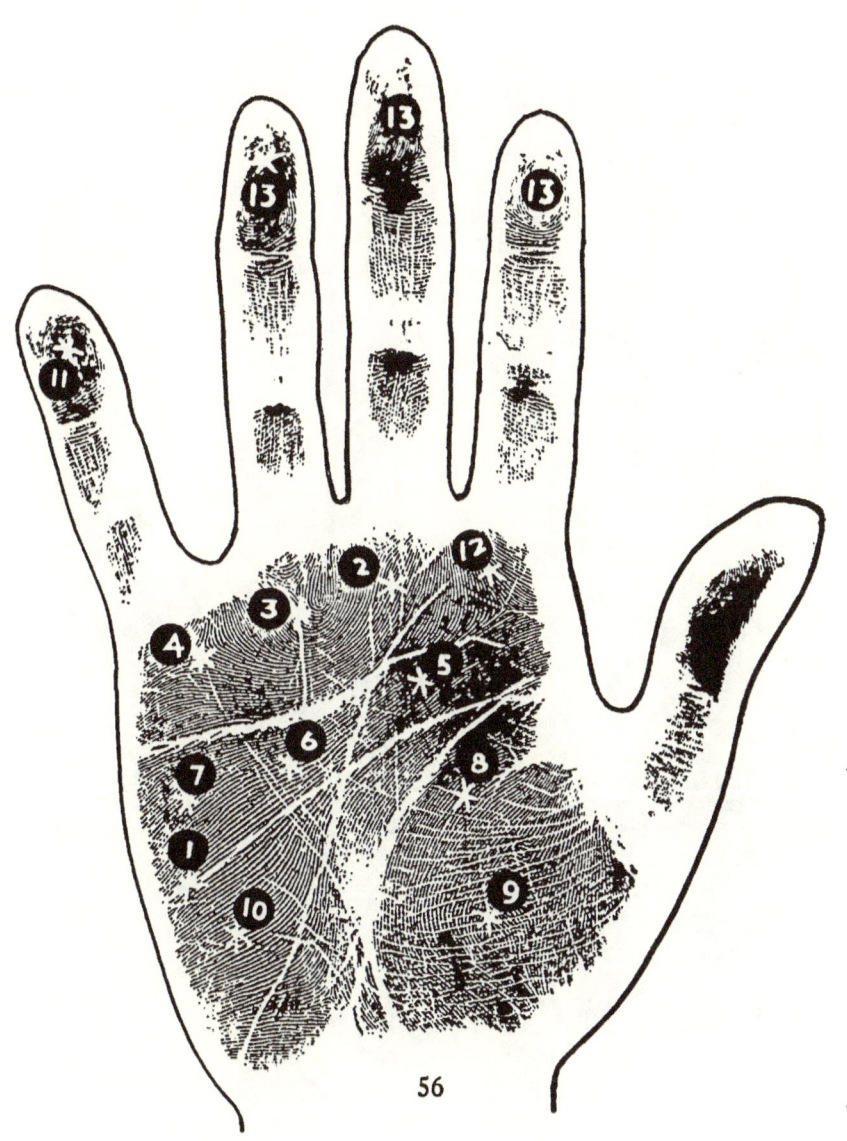

56

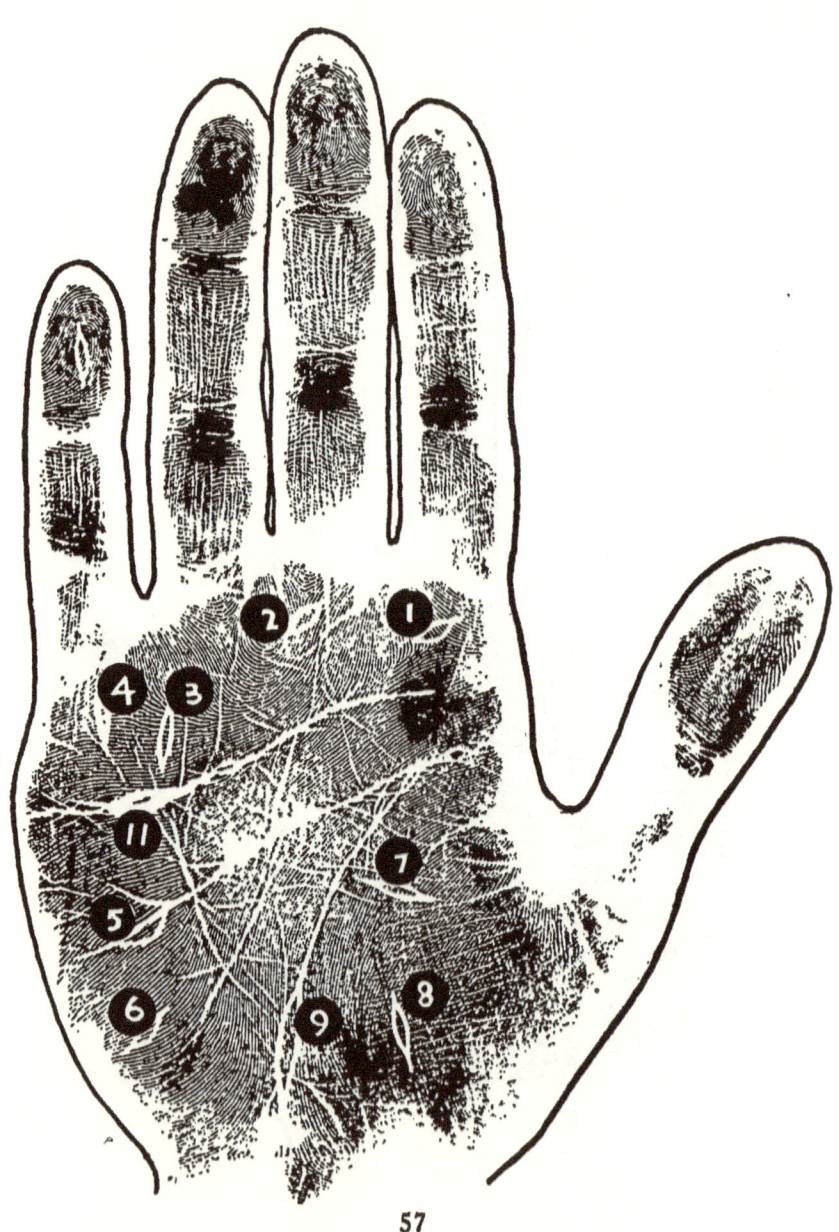

57

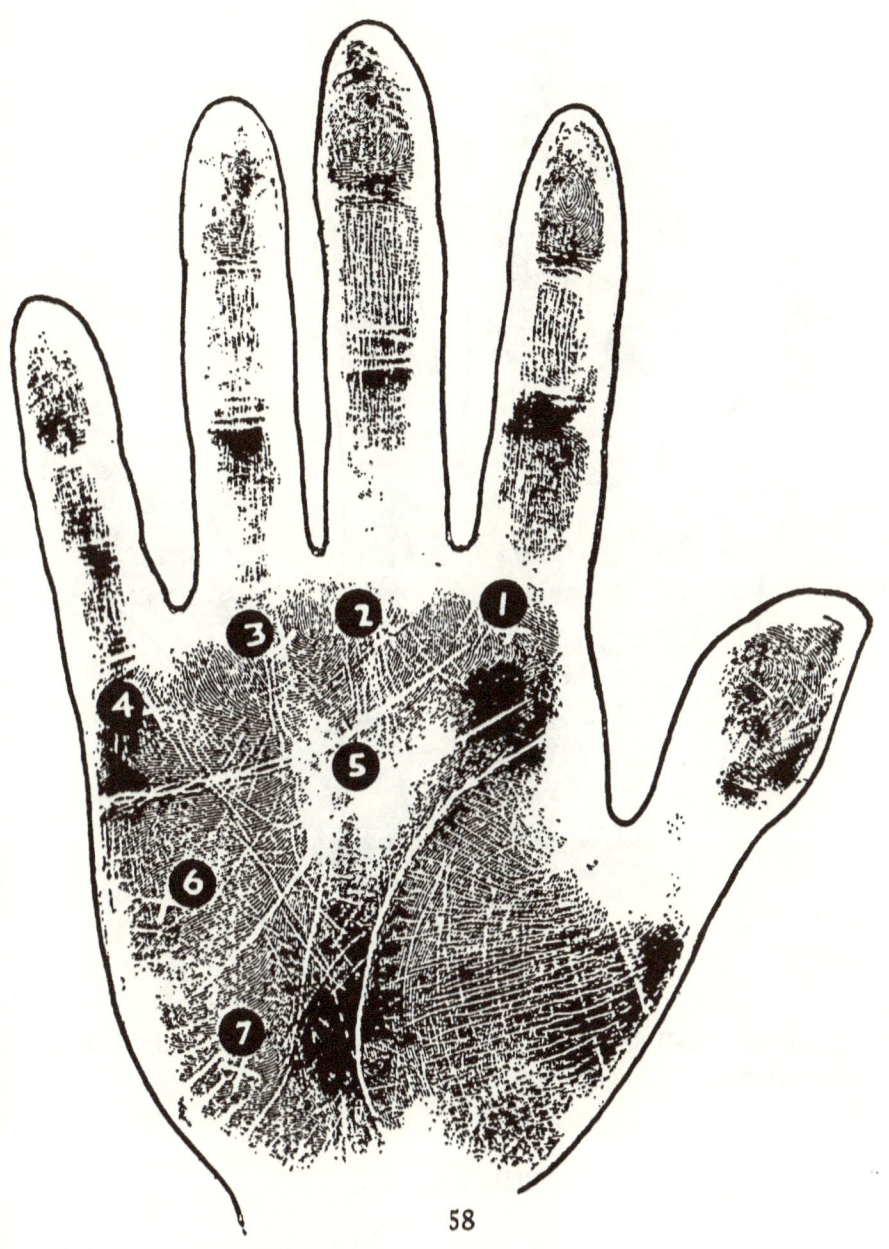

58

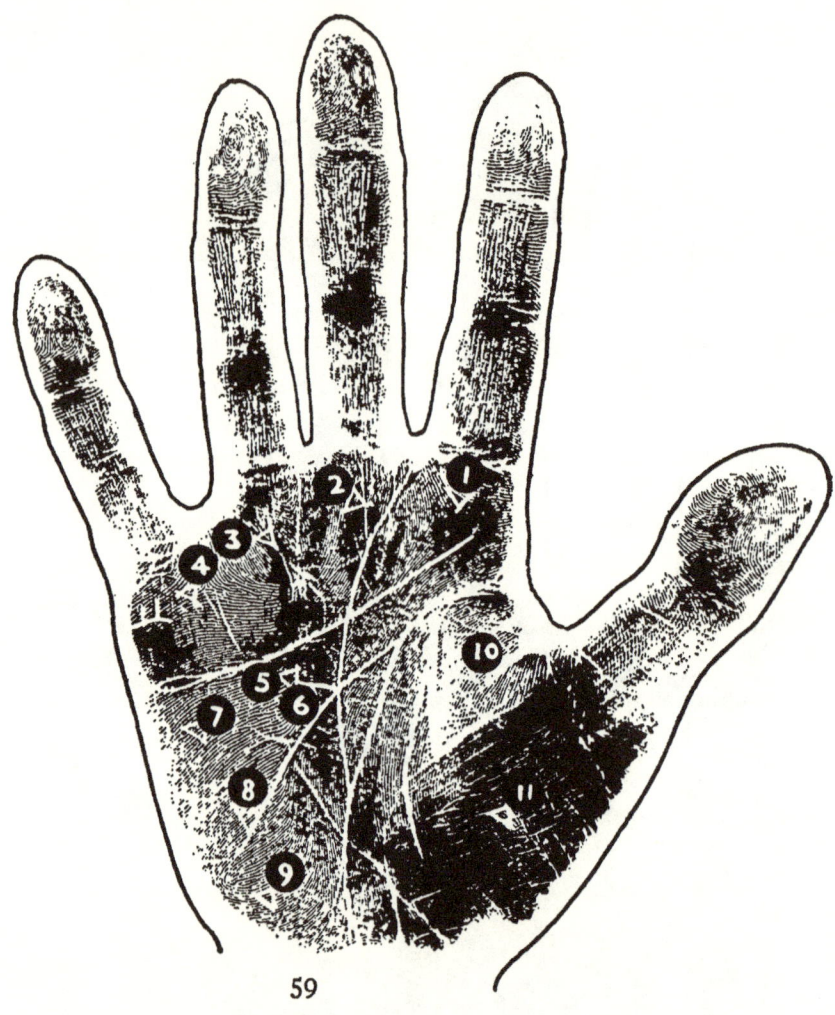

59

are marks of well developed sensory nerves, giving unusually delicate perception to the fingertips.

THE ISLAND

Unlike the star, an island (see plate 55) is never a fortunate sign.

When found in the body of a line, it reduces the positive implications of that line. When found in other positions, it usually weakens the promise of a mount or finger. On mount Jupiter (see plate 57, 1), an island shows some misfortune, possibly enmities, resulting from an overly ambitious, domineering nature. On mount Saturn (see plate 57, 2), an island produces a morbid, dark-tinged trend of thought. An island on or under mount Apollo (see plate 56, 3) shows loss of reputation through gossip or malicious interference by others. On mount Mercury (see plate 57, 4), an island means losses in business; on the heart line (see plate 57, 11), unfortunate loves; on the line of head (see plate 57, 5), either frequent headaches or some interference with the reason; at the end of the line of life (see plate 57, 9), some mystery, perhaps associated with the manner or circumstances of death; on mount Venus (see plate 57, 8), unhappy infatuations; on Mars positive (see plate 57, 7), fear of violence, though this may be temporary. An island on mount Luna (see plate 57, 6), unless it is accompanied by a very poor line of head or a weak thumb, can usually be counteracted. Its indication is of a disordered, fantastic imagination, and discipline will overcome it.

THE CROSS

The cross (see plate 55) may be either fortunate or the opposite, according to its position. Under the index finger (see plate 58, 1), it brings fulfillment to ambition. On mount Saturn (see plate 58, 2), it signifies a morbid disposition, though not so deep nor consistent a melancholia as that connoted by an island in this position. Under the Apollo finger (see plate 58, 3), a cross gives keen observation, invaluable to the student of human nature or the reporter. On mount Mercury (see plate 58, 4), a cross intensifies the keen business sense which goes with that finger. A cross on mount Mars, negative under Mercury (see plate 58, 6), ameliorates stubbornness. On mount Luna (see plate 58, 7), a cross shows a vivid imagination put to the use of self-deception, and on the plain of Mars, between the lines of head and heart (see plate 58, 5), a cross signifies a person fascinated by mysticism.

THE TRIANGLE

The triangle, which is usually found on one of the mounts, points up the special talents associated with that mount or with the finger of the same name. A triangle on mount Jupiter (see plate 59, 1) shows the ability to rule great masses of people. A triangle on mount Saturn (see plate 59, 2) counteracts the sombreness of that thoughtful finger and indicates melancholy successfully overcome. A triangle under the Apollo finger (see plate 59, 3) gives administrative ability in finance. Under the Mercury finger (see plate 59, 4), it shows executive powers in business. On Mars negative (see plate 59, 7), it manifests great spiritual resources. At the end of the line of head (see plate 59, 8), it gives the powers of sound reasoning to counteract too vivid an imagination. On mount Luna (see plate 59, 9), a triangle shows presence of mind in emergency; on Venus (see plate 59, 11), calmness and stability in love; on Mars positive (see plate 59, 5), social interests and abilities.

THE CIRCLE

The circle has but few connotations. I have often found it situated under the third finger or between the second and third fingers in the hands of singers or those who are gifted musically in other ways. At the base of mount Luna, a circle shows vivid dramatic imagination.

THE TRIPOD

A fork with two short even branches, like the base of a photographer's tripod seen sectionally (see plate 55) shows dramatic talent. I have found a formation of this shape on the lines of head, on the destiny line, on the Apollo line, or even on the line of heart of some of those who have made their mark behind the world's footlights or under the Kleigs. This is called a tripod.

THE SQUARE

A square (see plate 55) is always a sign of healing. When it binds a broken line together, it shows the overcoming of whatever originally caused the break. The square must be considered in relation to the position in which it appears. On a mount, it means protection from the negative connotations of that mount. On a line, it means preservation from ill health, from excesses, from poor choice in the selection of your career, protection from bad judgment in a love affair, or in business.

THE GRILLE

A grille, made up of many lines crossing in opposite directions, resulting in a sort of screen effect (see plate 55), may be found in any part of the hand, but it usually appears on a mount. The grille signifies difficulties and weaknesses in connection with the qualities associated with the particular mount on which it appears. On the mount of Mercury, a grille connotes indiscretion; on Apollo, vanity and danger of notoriety from too much seeking of the limelight; on Saturn, melancholia; on Jupiter, stiffnecked pride and a domineering nature.

SIGNIFICANCE OF THE SIGNS

Of course, the force of any of the incidental marks on a hand must, like everything else, be read in conjunction with the general indications of the hand—its shape, consistency, flexibility,—and especially in connection with the particular line or mount on which the mark occurs. An island, for example, on a line which is clear and bold both before and after its interruption by that unfortunate mark is not so threatening as an island situated in a line which is weak throughout its entire length, or much broken up after the appearance of the island.

My experience with hands leads me to differ with those authorities who deny all significance to such markings as the square, island, circle or grille. But I do agree with them that too arbitrary and specific a meaning can be read into them. The import of these signs must be arrived at through a balancing of all the factors appearing in the hand, and the interpretation placed upon them must never be given finality. The hand must always be regarded in a state of flux, just as is the personality as a whole. If you make a point of studying hands over a period of years, you will be surprised at the changes to be found in a person's hand as he grows and changes.

Chapter XVI. THE STRUCTURE OF THE HAND

WHEN the doctor looks at hands, what does he see? Certainly not only what we laymen behold, a moving part of the body having the power to grasp objects, move them, make them, change them; nor does he see just an appendage through which we can express ourselves, supplementing our powers of speech by gesture.

Underlying the doctor's professional glance at our hands is his knowledge of their structure and their functioning. First, he sees in the hand a part of the body whose development he can trace through the centuries. Though there are large gaps in the doctor's knowledge of evolution, which he has to bridge with guesswork and theory, he has a consistent explanation of the successive steps by which life in its simplest form—a tiny, undifferentiated bit of living matter—became more complicated. Cells of living matter became specialized in form and function. In the simplest forms, a single cell had limited and elementary powers of motion and feeling. That single cell combined the functions of eating, reproducing and reacting to outside stimuli. As the organism grew more complicated, special cells became different from their fellows. Certain ones took on the job of responding to outside impressions. These were nerve cells. Others took on the job of producing substances needed by the body. These were gland cells. Others had the work of contracting, or moving. These made up the muscle tissue.

The doctor sees all these cells at their work in the hand. Structurally, he sees a skeleton of small bones at the wrist, the carpal bones, and other small bones extended to make the fingers. These are the metacarpals and phalanges. The formation, the consistency, the size of these bones tell the doctor a story about the health of his patient.

Covering the bones, the doctor sees the muscular tissue, and it tells its story. And, carrying life into the hand, the doctor sees a system of blood vessels, part of the body's circulatory system. This tells the doctor still another story through the color and the temperature of the hand. The skin, to the doctor, is not just a thin, protective covering for the hand. It is made up of rows of cells—an outer layer, the epidermis, and an inner one, the derma (or corium). And in these rows he finds tiny glands and nerve cells.

The doctor knows that the hand is very highly endowed with sensory nerve cells, which take the messages of sensation to the brain. Then millions of other nerve cells receive the message back and pass it on to the muscular tissue. As the same stimulus is repeated over and over again, it beats an accustomed path through the central nervous system to the brain's cortex, and thus it is that we form our habits, learn to associate one thing with another, develop a memory.

The hand, probably as much or more than any other part of the body, is the destination of many of the complicated messages from the brain, for the hand can learn to do things which are far removed from simple reflex action or from instinctive reaction. The hand can learn to play the violin, to weave, to build houses, to paint, to mix chemicals. Is it any wonder that the hand records its owner's life in a living tapestry?

Just as the nerves form a telegraphic coordinating system governing movement and responses through the body, so do the gland cells influence the chemistry of the body. The two functions really cannot be separated, for the health and activity of certain glands, particularly the ductless or endocrine glands, influence the nerve responses. Take the thyroid gland, located in the throat region. This gland produces thyroxin, which can completely alter a person's temperament. Absence or deficiency of thyroxin will result in the storage of large amounts of fat. It will cause subnormal body temperature, a slower pulse, a general slowing of the body's living processes accompanied by mental and physical sluggishness. The hand will exhibit definite symptoms showing this thyroid deficiency. And excess of the thyroid hormone, which raises the tempo of living, increases the pulse rate and results in emaciation and nervous irritability, will also be indicated in the hand.

I am by no means urging that physicians should substitute hand analysis for the diagnostic methods which the science of medicine has developed throughout the centuries. But I do believe that the hands are an important diagnostic aid, the significance of which has been very largely overlooked by the practicing physician. Their value lies not only in the corroborating symptoms which they display and which give greater certainty to a diagnosis. They have still another, twofold contribution for medicine. First, I would transfer the prophetic powers which superstition has assigned to palmistry to the medical aspect of hand analysis. It is very true that conditions of the blood, the functioning of the circulatory system, of the glands, the resulting irritability of unresponsiveness of the nervous system, leave their mark in the hands often long before the abnormal condition has become sufficiently marked to be classed as a disease or illness. Thus, hands point to dangers threatening the health, and mark out particular classes of ailments to which a person is predisposed.

As our civilization becomes more complex, we deal more and more with substances which are injurious to our health. With the entrance of chemistry into industry, there has arisen a whole new series of ailments known as industrial diseases. In a sense, they are not entirely new to modern times, for certain processes go far back into history. In the dead civilizations of the past, laborers fell victim to lead poisoning, miners had special, mysterious illnesses, potters died of conditions not shared by other craftsmen. But the incidence and virulence of these self-induced diseases is multiplied by every new factory, increased by each new process, spread in every new mining town and manufacturing center. Millions of free men die or drag out their days in a half-death caused by what Pliny called the "slave diseases."

Physicians who have studied occupational diseases often find the earliest symptoms in the hands. Conditions which result in tuberculosis, wasting away of the tissues and energies of man, could be dealt with much earlier if factories installed regular physical checkups, including careful examination of their workers' hands, and took preventive measures where a new process was found to be hazardous.

Still another value which hands have for the physician is in the key they give to a patient's psychology. There are many theories why this is so. I have no definite answer to the mystery, except to suggest that the intimate connection of the hands with the functioning of the entire body gives the hands a sort of preview of the things which make us behave, not only like human beings, but like a particular human being, Jack Jones, or Jill Smith. Whatever the reason, I have found the hands an unusually accurate guide not only to the temporary attitude of a person toward life, but also to the more or less consistent outlook which runs like a main motif through all his actions. Since, in many diseases, the patient's psychological state is as important as his physiological, I think a study of the hands will give extremely valuable aid in their treatment. So long as man's self is the least understood phenomenon with which he has to deal, he ought certainly to use every means by which he can know himself better.

If this applies to diseases whose causes are organic and recognizable, how much more does it apply to functional conditions whose causes are obscure, buried in the complex whole. Hypochondria may range from the tantrums of a bored debutante to a self-induced paralysis. And the borderline between mental balance and unbalance, or emotional control and lack of it, gives us an unexplored region in human behavior where we must take direction from every guidepost our limited knowledge affords us.

Chapter XVII.   THE NAILS

ABNORMALITIES in shape, strength, texture, brittleness and color of the nails are accepted even by the most conservative of medicos as indicative of the body's condition. Already, there are nail symptoms which are hardly open to question. Interpretation of others is still somewhat controversial. I have found, however, that my opinion of a person's physical condition, in which study of the nails plays a

large part, is unusually accurate. I have examined hands and sub-
sequently checked my findings with a physician's diagnosis. On
more than one occasion, I have been able to point to definite dangers
menacing the health of an individual, and the treatment of the condition I discovered has in some cases prevented its becoming much
more serious. Where a case has already been diagnosed, a skeptic
might say that my guess was the result of telepathic communication,
but where mine was the original diagnosis, the only explanation
which satisfies reason is that the method I use is an accurate one.

The nail's shape in itself shows predispositions towards certain ailments and is a fairly good index to a person's general physical condition.

Long, oval-shaped nails (see plate 60) usually belong to those
whose physical constitution is weak. With nails of this oval shape are

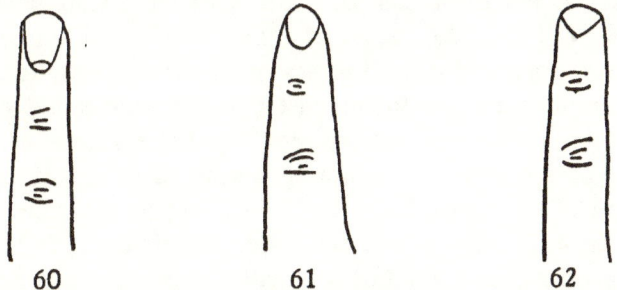

60   61   62

associated deficiencies of the blood—anemia, for example—and diseases of the respiratory system. A bluish color on nails of this type
is added evidence of anemia. The liability to pulmonary diseases is
perhaps as much due to lowered resistance, a result of malnourish-
ment and resultant anemia, as to any direct association between nails
of this shape and the lungs.

A short, neat, oval nail, without moons (see plate 61) is classed as
the cardiac type. Its color is usually bluish. This may signify an
organic defect of the heart. The same shape on a nail with moons
well-developed is often the accompaniment of functional disorders of
the circulatory system, palpitations or high blood pressure. A very
high arch in the nail supports the diagnonis of palpitations.

Short nails, very flat and broad at the tip but tapering into a
point at the base and thus giving a triangular effect (see plate 62)

are most often found on persons of highly nervous temperament. Such nails if accompanied by significant enlargement of the first phalanx may show an improperly functioning thyroid, but the indication is much too uncertain to be given credence by itself. At best, it can be looked upon as a diagnostic aid in pre-clinical illness, pointing out the inception of disease or a predisposition to certain conditions. White flecks show an aggravation of the nerves.

Throat weaknesses I have often found associated with nails shaped somewhat like the nervous type, that is, broad at the tip and pointed at the base. There is, however, this difference. The nail which goes with susceptibility to bronchial ailments is curved in outline, while the nervous nail has straight, flat contours.

The texture of the nail should be smooth. Heavy transverse ridging may be a warning of paralysis. Such consistent cross ridging of the nail is not to be confused with occasional transverse grooves. The latter are only the record of a minor indisposition in the past. They never foretell future illnesses or predispositions. In fact, they are so definitely related to the past that they indicate just how far back in time an illness has occurred by the distance of the ridge from the base of the nail. Allowing a span of about six months for the length of the entire nail—the time it ordinarily takes for a nail to grow its full length—you can judge the time which has elapsed since the ridge first grew into the nail.

Spots on the nail are signs of various kinds of disorders, though they are not very specific in their message. White spots show excess nervous irritability—the response of too many nerve cells to outside stimuli. You will generally find these little white speckles in the hands of excitable, tense persons. In children, the white spots are a warning for parents to work out a simple regimen of life with regular meals, regular sleeping hours, and regulation of the body functions. A change in the color of the spots to a pinkish or yellowish hue usually shows the return to good health. Dark spots, brown or blue, show some serious condition of the blood, possibly an infection or the presence of an inorganic poison.

The color of the entire nail is also significant. A healthy nail is pinkish, smooth and has a certain natural brilliancy. Irregular blotchings of pink and white are an index to poor blood condition, though beyond that, this symptom will not specify the nature of the condition. Very pale nails show lack of vitality, possibly a calcium deficiency, especially if the nail is soft. Bluish nails warn of poor circulation and, in women, of irregular functioning of the sex organs. A bluish nail bordered with a dark red outline is usually a sign of auto-intoxication, the accumulation of poisons because of faulty elimination.

A short, narrow nail, pale, very thin and much curved, is often found to accompany either calcium deficiency or incomplete calcium assimilation. Since the utilization of calcium in our bodies is closely connected with the endocrine glands, such nails are often a warning to look into the glandular functioning.

Short, broad nails having a bright, good color go with good vitality and health. Temporary ridges or spots may appear even in healthy nails, when a person is overworked, but the surface usually remains smooth.

Chapter XVIII. THE CONFORMATION AND SHAPE OF THE HAND AND ITS SIGNIFICANCE IN MEDICINE.

TO SAY that a thin, much-lined hand is the nervous type is not to repeat the superstitions of witch doctors and brewers of herbs. It is to recognize what I have already pointed out, that a person's temperament is directly dependent on the functioning of the endocrine glands and that the hand's general conformation is also affected by the same causes. Minute differences in the body's chemistry will greatly change its physical, mental and emotional reactions. The doctor sees the hand as an index to the totality of personality—not just in the narrow sense, but in the broader sense combining physiological and psychological aspects.

So far as the hand goes, any irregularity in size immediately arouses the doctor's suspicion. If the hands are noticeably large, the palms deepened, all the palmar eminences enlarged and the fingers stubby with the first phalanx having a slightly puffy appearance, the doctor will look for other symptoms of acromegaly, caused by imperfect functioning of the pituitary gland. This gland is a small body located on the ventral side of the fore-brain in all vertebrates. The ailments which result from abnormalities in the workings of this gland are often obscure and badly understood. In such case, the additional evidence which the hands offer ought certainly not to be neglected.

Diseases of the thyroid gland are also evidenced in the hand. In hyperthyroidism or myxedema, the metabolism of the entire body is thrown out of gear. This produces changes in the appearance of the skin, including the subcutaneous tissue lying directly under it. Since the thyroid gland also regulates some of the activities of the internal organs, such as the liver, and is responsible for the rate of absorption of fat in the body, faulty secretion by the thyroid gland causes accumulation of fatty tissue in certain parts of the body, usually in the face, the torso and the hands.

As the condition is aggravated, the face becomes over-developed and the hands take on a fat, pudgy look. Action of the entire system becomes sluggish and dull. The extreme condition of this disease produces a mental and physical torpor approaching idiocy. By careful administration of thyroid extract to patients suffering from the disease, the fat may be rapidly burned in the body: the sufferer loses weight; metabolism is restored to its proper rate; and, along with the disappearance of other symptoms, the hands usually assume their normal appearance.

When the body's calcium-phosphorous balance is disturbed, another noticeable change occurs in the hands. The cuticle becomes excessive in formation, and the skin around the nails, instead of being soft and pliable, becomes hard, dry and cracked. Defective "parathyroid" conditions may speed up this abnormal reaction. Often patients whose hands bear thick, dry cuticles like this are subject to rheumatic diseases and to arteriosclerosis, more commonly known as hardening of the arteries.

Diagnosis of chronic rheumatism is aided by the study of the hand's appearance, for the appendicular symptoms of rheumatism are quite definite. The knuckles are knobbed and swollen, sometimes painful, but they can easily be recognized by the knoblike protuberance of the joints. This is not to be confused with the knotty bone formation of a healthy large-jointed hand. Where there is a morbid condition of the joint, you will usually see the skin inflamed and stretched over the projecting articulations. There are also deformities and unnatural shapes of the hand associated with many other diseases, especially those of nerve involvements causing wasting away or overdevelopment.

The hands of older people are characterized by conditions peculiar to their age. There is the "pill-roller" hand, which assumes a position similar to that taken in rolling pills or cigarettes with the thumb and forefinger. This is symptomatic of paralysis agitans. Then, there is the condition known as "preacher's" or "benediction" hand. This usually accompanies inflammations of the brain-covering in the region of the cervical spine. In still other conditions, the hand takes on the appearance of an animal's claw, which indicates to the doctor that there is pressure on the nerve trunk or injury to the nerve centers in the spine.

The fingers' shapes have their role in the drama of health and disease. Very short clubbed and stubby fingers are frequently due to poor return circulation, the evidence of some cardiac or pulmonary involvement. Certain abnormalities in the fingers are so specifically associated with diseases affecting the entire body that they are called by the name of the disease. There are, for example, gouty fingers, syphilitic fingers and tuberculous fingers, each characteristic of the disease for which they are named. Others, just as specific in their diagnostic application, are known by terms descriptive of their appearance, like the baseball finger. It is my contention that careful study of the fingers' shapes would immeasurably add certainty to our present diagnostic methods. These are, after all, still largely based on experience and association with little or no actual proof underlying their application.

Chapter XIX. THE SKIN, LINES AND RIDGES IN THEIR APPLICATION TO MEDICINE

IN ADDITION to the formation, consistency and shape of the nails and of the hand as a whole, the skin of the hand will frequently give a clue to the type of malady to which a person may be subject. A warm, pliant skin, especially when it is excessively moist, points to the possibility of sexual abnormalities. This may take the form of overestimated sex impulses, even though the impulses are not given direct expression. In fact, inhibition sometimes intensifies the condition and leads to corollary diseases. Another possibility to be explored in connection with this type of skin is overactivity of the thyroid gland and the nervous excitation which is its accompaniment.

Very fine skin of normal temperature and moisture, covering flesh of firm, elastic consistency, shows a personality very close to normal except for a slight tendency towards greater than average sensitivity to nervous excitation.

The sort of person whose instinctive emotional responses are repressed, one in whom there is definite conflict between the primary impulse and its expression, can often be identified by a very dry, flaky skin. This, too, is indicative of improper functioning of the thyroid gland, usually lack of sufficient thyroid secretion. The coarser and lower in temperature this type of skin, the more certain is this diagnosis. Nervous energy lacking vigorous physical resistance characterizes this condition.

In diagnosing functional ailments, the physician has found that psychological aspects must play a larger and larger part in his considerations. Suggestion, auto-suggestion and hysteria are often accompanied by physiological symptoms which can scarcely be distinguished from actual disorders. In some cases, one leads to the other, as in self-induced paralysis where partial atrophy of unused muscles may result from disuse. Study of the formation of the line of head, of course in relation to the hand as a whole and to other symptomatic indications, aids in identification of neuroses or even of the more advanced psychoses.

For every maladjustment, there are previous indications, identifying the type of person and the type of mental unbalance to be expected of him. The wide swings from one extreme to another characteristic of manic-depressive insanity find their expression in the hand, and the duality of the schizophrenic is also shown there. Where the headline itself is of poor quality, feathered, broken or chained, too vivid an imagination and tendencies to melancholia are almost predestined to result in unbalance. Therefore, an inferior headline with a branch swinging sharply down and penetrating deeply on to the mount of Luna can be taken as corroborating indication of this type of insanity.

In a hand with a very poor headline, if the mount of Venus is not well developed and the mount of Saturn is dominant, morbid hallucinations may occur in early life. In such cases, proper therapeutic measures are able to stabilize the mind, but opposition or attempts at suppression aggravate the condition.

The various degrees of subnormal mentality are usually coupled with hands which have no marked abnormalities but rather a generally subnormal index. The will phalanx of the thumb will be undeveloped. Reasoning powers will be lacking. Emotional responses will be very limited. Aesthetic sensibilities will be of the simplest, though not necessarily entirely absent.

In the hand of someone who is mentally subnormal, we usually find a wide-sloping line of head made up entirely of islands or little hairlines. This formation is characteristic of the congenital idiot or imbecile, usually quite harmless and childish, but never able to develop into normal adulthood.

When such subnormality is due to glandular dysfunction, symptoms of that condition will, of course, also be present.

When unbalance is added to such a subnormal hand, the vicious concomitants of insanity can be expected. There may be signs of sexual abnormality to complicate lack of mentality. The head line will often be made up of short branches running in all directions. A number of lines may start inside the line of life on mount Mars and cross the hand to the opposite mount of Mars. The nails on this type of hand are generally very short and red, the fingers crooked.

Aside from its general quality and appearance, the skin of the palmar surface shows tiny ridges assuming definite patterns. Their nature cannot be determined definitely except by microscopic examination, for the formations are too minute to be differentiated by the naked eye. Such an examination is much more accurately made from a handprint, which reveals the ridges with greater clarity than does the hand itself.

The pattern is formed only on the outer layer of the skin. Nevertheless, it is extremely significant in the study of hands in connection with the body's health. Normally, the ridges are clear and distinct. Breaks, dots, points and other malformations are indicative of diseased conditions. But it is important to differentiate between breaks in the actual pattern and the breaks caused by disease.

Two kinds of disease conditions are most easily distinguished through malformations in the ridges of the palmar skin: bacterial infections and absorption of inorganic poisons. Apparently the invasion of the body by hostile micro-organisms or foreign substances produces chemical changes which cause characteristic alterations in the skin. The ridge pattern itself is left unaltered, but the lines which form it are changed in appearance.

In malaria, I have noticed that the ridges just under the line of head are interrupted by minute, white dots, not large enough to break the ridge line. In an enlarged print or under the microscope, they look like tiny white speckles scattered inside the ridge line.

Intestinal infections show up as irregular breaks in the ridges and pieces gouged out of their edge, giving the ridges a crenellated outline. Non-malignant ulcers are associated with lack of definition in the ridging of the skin caused by irregular interruptions and a sort of featheriness in the ridges' outlines.

Many fine dots along the line of heart are indicative of heart disease. When these dots increase, clustering in crowded bunches at any one point, there is usually also a break or weakening of the heart line at that point, presaging danger of cardiac failure. Muscular deterioration of the heart may be shown by a melting of the ridges under the heart line into clusters of fine dots.

The great variety of toxic conditions which may originate in the intestines is accompanied by as great a variation of ridge malformations, usually situated just under the line of head and near its termination. Locating the seat of a troublesome systemic infection is thus aided by study of the hand. Diagnosis of the nature of the infection requires careful consideration of all the symptoms, including analysis of the palmar ridges.

One of the discoveries of modern medicine is that simple rheumatism, which used to be blamed for every little-understood inflammation or pain and ache, is really a complex of widely divergent factors. Dental infections, cardiac weaknesses, faulty diet—all may play their part in causing the disease. Naturally, the palmar indications differ with the nature of the ailment, and it is my belief that complete understanding of their significance will go far toward identifying the conditions underlying symptoms generally classed as rheumatism. This, in turn, will point to the specific treatment and possible cure.

Where the palm gives evidence of a functional disorder of the intestinal tract, where there are many small islanded formations and tiny perpendicular lines from the outer edge of the hand in towards the center of the palm, acute rheumatism may be looked for. In arthritis, there is always some indication of bacterial intoxication. Usually the life and head lines will be feathered with minute dots, giving them a light, fluffy appearance. Even the fate line is sometimes so marked.

Perhaps it is in early identification of the dread disease, cancer, that study of the hand will have its greatest value to medicine. All authorities are agreed that early diagnosis and treatment in the first stages are essential. Yet the first symptoms are often so vague that they are passed over as of no consequence and medical care is postponed until too late.

Authorities find that the hand quite definitely indicates the predisposition to cancer, and early stages of the disease can readily be detected. Malignant growth can be identified by the typical malformation of the palmar ridges. Seen under the microscope, these show regular breaks made by clean transverse cuts at fairly even intervals, giving the ridges the general appearance of rows of tiny soldiers. This cancerous formation is almost always placed just under the end of the line of head.

In the same way, the hand will show characteristic deviations from normal surface markings for diabetes, disorders of the genital system, kidneys, liver or nerve and circulatory machinery. It is hardly within the scope of this book to enlarge on these symptoms, nor is it the place of a layman to theorize too extensively about the nature and cause of disease. On one thing I want to caution the reader. Proper diagnosis cannot be made through the hands alone, certainly not through casual perception of a single indication in the hands. A careful student of the hand must balance all the facts presented to arrive at even the most tentative hypothesis. A physician will still need to place his reliance mainly on the symptoms he knows. I am only suggesting that he add the symptoms appearing in the hand to those he is accustomed to study and accept in evidence. I believe that the additional information thus gained will give some measure of guidance, especially in the determination of predispositions and the identification of diseases in their very early stages.

Chapter *XX*. TYPES OF FINGERPRINTS

THE one use to which study of the hands has been put with thorough scientific method is in fingerprinting for the purposes of identification. Knowledge that individual fingerprints differ from each other is no new thing. The Chinese were aware of this fact many thousands of years ago and made use of it as a means of verifying important documents.

It is only recently, however, that the western world has adopted fingerprinting as an aid to its police work and in keeping track of records embracing large numbers of persons. The master criminal identification file which the Federal government has built up in Washington contains what is probably the largest collection of fingerprints in the world, each classified according to type, and no two exactly alike.

This is the basis of the fingerprint identification system—that there are no two sets of fingerprints in the world which are exactly alike and further that each record is a permanent one. Though the hands change in the shape even of their bony structure, though the strong, muscular hand of a youth will become flabby and corded with age, though the individual lines and markings of the palm may be completely altered in the course of a lifetime, the design made by the papillary ridges on the fingertips remains the same throughout life. If the ridges are mutilated, they grow back in the identical pattern. The ridging in the palm is subject to slight alterations, more in the nature of its lines (as I have indicated in the chapter about the medical application of hand analysis) than in the formation of the pattern, but the palm, too, can be used for identification purposes.

How is it possible to classify and use the fingerprints if they grow in such infinite variety? The explanation is that, though they vary in detail, the designs on our fingertips all conform to a few basic patterns. They are all evolved from the ridging which grows in concentric circles on the cushion pads which animals have on their feet.

TYPES OF FINGERPRINTS

Nearest to this design of concentric circles is the *true whorl* (see plate 63). Next is the *spiral whorl,* which is the beginning of the design breakdown with its tendency for the ridges to straighten out. The spiral whorl is usually composed of two ridges starting at a

63

central point and widening out into ever larger spiral circles, like the vortex of a whirlpool.

The third design in the ridge patterns is the *loop formation* (see plate 64). In the first of these, the *double loop* type, the two ridges at the center of the spiral whorl have lengthened into two U-shaped loops, opening in opposite directions, and the ridges of the fingertip flow in rounded arcs from these two loops as their center. The *single loop* is a still further step in the process of widening and unwinding the center of the whorl design. It differs from the double loop only in that one of the loops has disappeared, but its lines still follow each other closely from their common center.

The fourth design is that in which the U-shaped loops open out into a wider arch curving about an upright in the *tented arch* formation (see plate 65). Then there is the ordinary arch (see plate 66), and finally there is the composite form which, as its name indicates, combines the ridges in loops, whorls or arches (see plate 67).

64

These basic patterns, the whorl with its variations, the loop, the arch, the tented arch and the composite are the basis for our system

65   66

of identification by fingerprints. In the millions of fingers in this world, there may be individual digits—a very few—which are exactly alike, having the same number of ridge lines, of the same thickness, with breaks, changes of direction and curves all exactly duplicated.

But there will be no two hands in which the ten digits are all exactly the same and in the same combination.

Though criminal identification is still the best known use of finger-prints, many other applications are now coming into practice. A few banks have substituted fingerprints for a witnessed cross as authorization from depositors who cannot write. Similarly, the govern-

67

ment requires fingerprints from all who entrust money to the Postal Savings system. In these two cases, institutions which have accepted responsibility wish to safeguard themselves by making sure of the identity of those they deal with. The protection extends to both the institution and the depositor.

Important documents may be signed by fingerprint rather than by pen. In this connection, if the object is to prevent fraud, a signature ought certainly to accompany the print on wills, deeds or similar papers, for it is obviously much simpler to obtain an involuntary print from the hand than to force a person to sign documents. Prints from the hands of a dead man, an unconscious one, or one who was under physical constraint might easily be obtained.

Other objections can also be raised, not to the use of fingerprints for identification, but to their use for oppression. The fingerprinting of employes by hotels, factories, mills has been used in industrial warfare to exclude union men from employment.

Yet these objections are not to fingerprinting *per se,* as a means of identification, but to its misuse in the hands of certain agencies. The benefits to be derived from fingerprint records of everyone are immense. Hospitals have been known to mix babies at their birth. The instances of such confusion are rare, but think of the anguish of even one pair of parents who will never be certain if the child they have is really their own. Law cases, claims on inheritances, various impostures have resulted. Handprinting at birth would completely eliminate such unsolvable riddles of identity, for with the print record of a new-born child could be taken an impression from the mother's hand.

What of the foundling babies, abandoned to the cold care of institutions while parents or other relatives are perhaps seeking to find them again? What of lost children, found by the police, whose description, bearing and childish tricks are advertised in the press, but never with such accuracy that parents feel completely relieved of doubt until they actually see their child again. What of the runaways? Publication of their handprints would lead to immediate identification. Handprint records would certainly speed the hunt for kidnaped children and quickly dispose of those false leads which mark every widely publicized case.

Many institutions have come to realize the value of finger and handprints. Maternity hospitals, finding that the tiny ridges on a baby's fingertips are too minute to make clear impressions, take prints of the foot. Footprints, however, do change more or less during the course of a lifetime. Because of this, Dr. Gilbert Palmer Pond has evolved a means which provides identification for life, using prints of an infant's palm. The ridging on the eminences of the palm is usually coarser than that on baby's fingertips, and such hospital impressions supply a means of identification which can be used for a lifetime. For absolute certainty, however, supplementing a baby's palm print with impressions of the fingertips taken at school age is advisable.

At the end of this book you will find sheets of sensitized hand-impression paper. One use to which you can put these sheets is as a sort of new family bible. Instead of recording the signatures of all the members of your family, you can here collect their handprints;

but I shall discuss this in greater detail in a later chapter which gives directions for the making of impressions.

I had one experience which brought the value of family handprint records home to me with great force. True, coincidence played an important part in the occurrence, yet without the aid of handprints, coincidence could not have effected its story-book work. My story begins a few years ago, when a woman of prominent family came to see me. The story she told me was a surprising one. Fifteen years before, she had married a young man of good family. His addiction to drink did not come as a complete surprise to her, but the extent of his failing did. Normally a thoughtful, rather moody person, her husband became quarrelsome and even violent when drunk. His weakness took more and more of a hold on him as time wore on. Had it not been for her infant son, she would have left her husband.

After two years of marriage, a particularly violent scene brought things to a climax. She threatened to have him forcibly committed and given a cure. He retaliated with violence, and she had to flee for her life. Unfortunately, her parents, to whom she immediately went for aid, were not at home, and she paced up and down the hallway for hours awaiting their return. As soon as they could, a family group rushed over to her unhappy home to take the child, but it was already too late. The house was empty except for the servants who had returned to find both the year-old boy and his father gone.

Of course they searched. At first, wishing to keep the tragedy from being made public, they hired private detectives. Then, in desperation, they appealed to the police. But for months, no one could find a trace of the missing pair. You can imagine the mother's agony. She had endured humiliation, even violence, from her husband for the sake of the child only to have her son taken from her. Worst of all was the uncertainty. Her waking moments were haunted by pictures of the baby, cold, neglected, hungry. Her dreams repeated the scenes with terrifying realism.

At last there was a gleam of hope. The police picked up the husband in a small Pennsylvania town. The entire family rushed West to see him. When they arrived, they found a shivering skeleton of a man tossing in the last stages of delirium tremens. The hospital gave no hope of life and no prospect of a rational word before death.

Fifteen years passed—fifteen years of constant search, of occasional hope, of ultimate despair.

There was little I could do. Naturally, I did not know where the child was. As much to bolster up the mother's spirits as for any useful purpose, I asked whether she had an impression of her baby's hand, telling her that such a print would at least help identify the boy if she ever found him.

At first she said no—she had never thought of having the child's handprint recorded. Then, suddenly, she recalled a series of tiny prints on the wall beside the crib, where the baby had steadied his first attempts to stand. The child's room had never been touched since the tragic night when it was emptied of its little occupant.

We rushed over to examine it. By a chemical process, I brought out the impressions on the wall and had photographs of them made. I studied the prints very carefully, trying to comfort the mother with all the information I could give her about her son. From the hand, I formed a picture of a very intelligent, well-balanced youth whose inheritance from his unhappy father was completely overshadowed by the good qualities with which his mother had endowed him. "Wherever he is," I told the unhappy mother, "I am sure that he is someone you could be proud of."

Though the handprint did not tell us where the missing boy was, it gave his mother renewed hope. With her new means of identification as an aid, she began a systematic search of orphanage records, tracing the careers of boys who had been sent out into the world. Strangely enough, it was not she, with her careful work, who discovered the boy. It was I, and quite by accident.

Many months had passed without my hearing from her. I was lecturing in Akron, Ohio, and was scheduled to address the high-school graduating class. The students, now preparing to take on the responsibilities of adulthood, were anxious to know the stories in their hands, and I agreed to look at all their prints, saying a brief word about each.

One impression among the many struck me as familiar. I thought that I had analyzed it before and, calling out the boy's name which was written on the impression paper, I asked whether I had already told him about his hand. He said that I had not.

Yet the print was not a strange one. I knew I had seen it before. I have a very peculiar memory. Some of you remember faces. Others can recall a person's name even after years of separation and only casual acquaintance. I am that way with hands. I never forget an interesting hand, and even more usual ones stay in my mind for a long time.

I asked the boy to speak to me after the exercises and learned that he was an adopted son, taken to an orphanage by the New Jersey family with whom his father had boarded him, rescued from there by his present foster parents. Even then I did not guess the truth, but on the train returning to New York I continued to study the boy's handprint. Suddenly, the little imprint we had taken off a white wall next to a baby's crib was pictured in my mind. I was not yet sure. Certainty awaited my actual comparison of this new print with the photograph I had in my files. A half hour's study of the two hands, and I was convinced.

The rest I need not tell you in detail—how I called the anxious mother, how we traced the movements of this boy from the time he was left a nameless boarder to the day I chanced on him in Akron, how all the other evidence upheld my certainty. You can imagine the mother's joy and the son's happiness at finding his own family.

A handprint record is also immensely valuable in connection with the aged and the sick. Have you not often read in the papers of men and women picked up wandering in the streets, unable to remember their names, their addresses, their occupations, or anything which could be used to restore them again to their families?

I recall one instance, which recently came to my attention, of an elderly woman who was led out of a large New York department store at closing time. She appeared to be a person of culture and refinement, accustomed to care and thoughtfulness from others. A victim of amnesia, she had forgotten what brought her to the store, who she was or where she came from. Institutions gave her their comfortless hospitality while her frantic family in another city appealed to the police, to travelers' aid societies, to welfare agencies, and even to hired private detectives. They spent terrifying hours examining unidentified bodies in morgues and studying photographs of other old women, picked up without name or associations. Only the restoration of her memory finally brought this grandmother and her family together again. Think of the suffering which might have been avoided had her family been able to send her fingerprints to police and hospitals all over the country.

Just to get an idea of the magnitude of the riddle of unsolved identity to which fingerprints would yield an answer, consider the lost and found statistics of Paris. Yearly, thousands of men, women, young boys and girls come to Paris and are never heard of again. In 1935, according to police records, almost sixteen thousand persons were reported "missing" in France's capital. These include husbands who have deserted their families, mothers who have left children, runaway boys and girls, old, young and middle-aged, the sick and the well, the lonely and the sorely missed, the honest and the crooked —on second thought, not the crooked, for criminals' trademarks are on record in the files of the Paris Sureté, just as American felons' are in Washington.

And these amazing figures apply to a city where everyone is required to register and carry papers of identification. In this country, the numbers are even more astounding. The New York City Missing Persons Bureau is now burdened with over thirty thousand identification cases each year. Eight thousand dead are buried every year in New York's potter's field, some because their families are unable to meet funeral expenses, but many more because they met death in accidents and were never identified. Meantime, their families' grief is continually renewed by uncertainty. The sparsely populated county of Los Angeles in California reported for one year over one hundred amnesia victims unidentified and consequently committed to institutions.

These figures apply to representative cities in normal times. In fire, flood and earthquake, the number of unidentified victims is appalling. Children, separated from their families, are never reunited with them. The dead and the injured are unclaimed. Bereaved families are in doubt for years about the fate of their loved ones. When the Ohio River overflowed its banks and routed thousands out of their homes, scattering family units, when the Morro Castle burned, when San Francisco was devastated by fire and quakes, rescue workers spent harrowing hours tracing the identity of living and dead; and anxious families waited, often for news which never came.

The government recognized the aid which fingerprinting would give when it ordered impressions made of all enlisted men in the world war. For this reason, the number of missing and unknown soldier dead was much cut down.

I would certainly not favor compulsory fingerprinting of everyone. In the first place, compulsion in such matters is hardly in the spirit of a democratic country; in the second, as I have said, records of this sort might very well be misused. But that does not mean that use of fingerprints and handprints for identification need be postponed until a new society eliminates man's oppression of man. On the contrary, private records made by yourself for your own use are today both feasible and of untold value.

Chapter XXI. CHILD TRAINING

IN DISCUSSING the application of hand analysis to vocational guidance, I wish first to take issue with the neat tabular classifications by which palmists used to assign a person to life as baker, broker, soldier or prima donna by virtue of a single indication of the hand. Nothing like that is possible. In prescribing a life's work, we must be as open minded and exact as a physician in prescribing a cure for diabetes. Tables sweepingly recommending certain vocations to hands of a given conformation are comparable to the medicine man's cure-all, and quack remedies in this field can be just as disastrous as in medicine.

I do not mean that hands are of no value in choosing your vocation. On the contrary, careful hand analysis, in my opinion, is an important branch of both psychology and physiology, or of the combined science which will some day probably take their place. To date, those systems of vocational guidance which lay claim to any scientific basis use the methods and content of both these sciences—psychology which deals with the workings of man's more or less intangible processes, and physiology which deals with the tangible, physical evidences of his functioning. Study of hands, with its bearing on both the mental or psychic aspect of man and on the medical or physical, should certainly be a part of all efforts to fit round pegs into round roles, square pegs into square holes. Study of man must precede proper direction of him, whether by himself or by others, and the hands, I have found, are a sure aid in man's study of man.

In my opinion the time to begin vocational training is in childhood. During the formative years, talents may be either developed naturally or twisted into unhealthy channels Though specialized training should usually be postponed until much later, a general direction should be decided upon quite early in life.

In this connection, it is necessary for parents to take a most objective point of view. Too often, I have seen promising children ruined because parents insisted on living their lives for them. That is not at all what I mean by early training. Where choice between various methods and subjects of study is required, the child's aptitudes and strength should be the guides. Certainly not the parents' ambition.

If a child's hand is much lined and flabby in consistency, you will find nervous excitability far beyond what is normal for a young person. Of course, glandular disturbances may be the cause, but parental mistakes, overindulgence, lack of regularity, bad temper in the parents, are almost sure to be an aggravating factor.

When, in a much-lined hand, the life line and the line of head are joined for a considerable distance, you have a timid child, dependent on others for encouragement. Such a child needs to be given self-reliance. He requires tranquility in the home and the companionship of others of his own age. If the headline is of good quality, he may be mentally precocious, yet arrested in his development because he is afraid to venture. Long, pointed fingers increase the sensitive responsiveness.

A child whose head and life lines are wide apart in both hands, who has firm unlined palms, will require cautious management. His independence should not be curbed, but impulsiveness and recklessness will need to be modified.

From a child's hand you can tell whether the wonderful stories which all children recount as true are the products of a vivid imagination, of illogical thinking, or of a wish to impress you or to excuse himself. The one characteristic should be cultivated, the other tendencies can be cured. From the child's hand you can determine how heavy a burden of study and physical exertion he is able to bear. You can also pick the natural aptitudes to be developed usefully and find the lacks which should be supplemented. A child with very short fingers can be taught method, though he should never be forced to spend his life at work which requires minute care for success. A child with long, straight fingers will not usually need to be trained in orderliness, but he may require that his interests be broadened.

When, in a child's hand, the line of head is broken or full of islands, it denotes some weakness of the brain. Often such a child will appear extremely intelligent, keen, full of curiosity, absorbing knowledge quickly and outdistancing his playmates at school. But concentration and memory will frequently be lacking, and a child with this type of headline requires careful supervision. He is likely to have great mental activity of a disorganized nature, combined with physical weakness. Therefore, he should be built up physically and at the same time restrained and directed in his studies and reading.

A line of head, curving far down towards the wrist and connected at its origin with the line of life, is characteristic of extremely irritable and temperamental children. This formation indicates a lively imagination, nervous excitability and delicate health.

A child having a very soft palm, pointed fingers and a sloping line of head is usually dreamy, inactive and somewhat indolent. Training in sports will do much to counteract the bad tendencies of this nature. A child with a very narrow palm is likely to be selfish. Group play, development of communal interests and sharing of his possessions are to be encouraged in such a child. Fingers spread very wide apart usually go with generosity, mental independence and lack of conventionality. In a child with such a hand, there must be careful analysis of the relative strength of the other factors. Too great unconventionality in the hand of a sentimentalist and weakling will lead to bohemianism without accomplishment. On the other hand, we owe much of our progress to persons who were not awed by the conventions of thought and manners.

It seems to me that hands are of especial importance in the training of children because many natural gifts are not otherwise apparent until much later in life. So long as an Albert Einstein can fail in school mathematics, we must look for other means of guiding ourselves in child training than merely the school record and behavior in the home. The study of hands ought to be one of those means.

Chapter XXII. ADULT VOCATIONAL GUIDANCE

SPECIALIZATION is the keynote of present-day vocations. For greater efficiency, man has subdivided even the physical labor of roadbuilding or the manufacture of an automobile into many processes with special machinery and special operators assigned to each. As for the sciences and humanities, our fund of knowledge is adding to itself such detail that one man is expected to master only a small fraction of the tremendous whole. Physicians have divided the body into tens of little bits, and doctors are ear specialists, eye specialists, abdominal surgeons, dermatologists. The general practitioner is almost extinct. Whereas the ancients produced men who could speak authoritatively about the movements of astral bodies, the plant life of the earth, the mental processes of man, the conventions of art, literature and drama; today a man does well indeed to become expert in but a single branch of one science. You have electro-physicists, physicists who deal only in the dynamics of wave mechanics, physicists who spend their lives studying radioactivity. Each devotes years to training for his profession. Theoretically, a mistaken choice is not uncorrectable, but it is often practically so. Men who might have been great statesmen are forced by their families or by some mistaken boyhood sentimentality to study and become unhappy and unsuccessful surgeons. Women who might compete with men in adventurous activities are condemned because of family pressure to lives in quiet, "womanly" occupations.

I do not want to take too unreal an attitude about our ability to pick and choose our life's work. I fully realize that poverty and lack of education, the necessity to go to work very young and all such very real circumstances interfere with our freedom to become all we are capable of being. Certainly, a person planning his future will need to consider the trends in modern industry and professions and not choose a certain type of work which has been superseded by newer methods. Certainly he will have to figure on the labor market, the supply of trained persons in relation to the abundance or scarcity of jobs in a particular field. Yet, to the extent that self-knowledge will help in adjusting people to conditions as they exist or in changing those conditions, to that extent will hand analysis be a real aid in vocational guidance.

To begin with, let us classify the vocations, though I shall make no attempt to be all-inclusive in my list. There are certain occupations which require method, order and precision above all else. Accounting, bookkeeping, office management, various kinds of clerking, laboratory work in chemistry or physics, secondary research, the keeping of records, historical, geological, ethnological research, administration, the law, in its less spectacular aspects, even the adventurous callings like soldiering and navigation require discipline and order. For patience and method, look especially to long, straight fingers. If they have square tips, expect practicality in addition, and little imagination. Long, squaretipped fingers are ideal for the bookkeeper or record clerk.

Long, tapering fingers, provided that the thumb is strong enough, and mount Jupiter prominent enough to give leadership, might be excellent for a government administrative officer. The length of his fingers would give him the patience and methodical approach necessary for dealing with endless details. The tapering fingers would provide sufficient sensitiveness and intuition to facilitate his dealings with others, to help him gauge the public temper. A strong thumb and firm hand would give him energy and determination, lack of which is the most outstanding fault of long, tapering fingers. Mount Jupiter would add qualities of leadership and ambition. For statesmanship, as contrasted with efficient government clerking, a wide palm ought also to provide the breadth of outlook and energy of the spatulate shape, and the line of head should be of good quality, preferably straight and well-balanced.

Short fingers are usually associated with a larger, more comprehensive point of view than is permitted by the long-fingered preoccupation with details. Among the short-fingered occupations, I would list promoters, publicists, financiers, investment bankers, bridge builders (though not the draftsmen and subordinate architects and engineers who figure stresses and compute the arches and suspensions), theatrical entrepeneurs, advertising experts, traders, adventurers, aviators, and so on. Short-fingered, vigorous hands, in which the mental aspects are little developed usually belong to those who work at out-door occupations calling for considerable physical energy.

The hand of great dexterity will usually be neither exceptionally short- nor long-fingered. Skilled mechanics, surgeons, operators of precision machines, cabinet makers, manicurists, watchmakers, embroiderers, barbers, sculptors, pianists, typesetters—these will generally have fingers of moderate length, and the other indications of the hand will show how the manual dexterity can be put to use. A long, thin second phalanx and prominent base on the thumb often indicate the accurate touch so necessary to the surgeon, dentist and skilled mechanic.

While the length of the fingers will give some indication of the general method of working and thinking natural to a man, the fingertips will greatly modify that preliminary finding. It is a safe assumption to assign sensitivity and intuition to pointed and tapering tips, practically to square ones, and energy to spready ones. The various combinations of differently shaped tips with fingers of different lengths will be even more significant than the story of either the fingers or the tips alone.

I think, however, that I can permit myself one generalization in connection with the various shapes of fingertips. Persons who have many dealings with others, whose success is dependent on their judgment of others and on tact and intuition, such as interviewers in employment agencies, head waiters, actors, teachers, claim adjusters, salesmen, contact men of all kinds, welfare workers, beauty operators, decorators, hotel managers—such persons should have the majority of their fingertips of tapering shape. Those whose work is largely practical and whose relations with coworkers are more or less impersonal can safely have squarish fingertips. Those who must dominate others have spatulate tips.

From the tips and fingers, we can form a rough picture of the kinds of work for which a man is fitted. Of course, to divide vocations by rigid lines is both incorrect and misleading. A mining engineer, assigned to supervise a new development in unexplored mountain regions, will require method and precision to make assays, to figure engineering problems. He will need tact, ingenuity, understanding and authority to deal with a strange people. He should have daring and physical energy and endurance. His hand would have to be a mixed hand, yet with certain traits outstanding.

The writer, the lawyer, the public speaker, the preacher, the newspaper reporter, the salesman, the auctioneer, the canvasser, the interpreter, the translator, need strong development of the Mercury finger. This finger governs verbal facility, whether of the spoken or written word. Yet an easy flow of words by no means makes either the great author or the great speaker; nor even the successful and aggressive salesman. Each occupation requires other gifts besides. For each of these professions there is no one ideal combination of handmarkings, representing combinations of talents; there are many. And for almost every hand there is more than one fitting avenue of expression. Your hand will not so much tell you the one and only way by which you may succeed and be happy as indicate the paths by which you cannot, and also, show you a number by which you might.

As illustration, I should like to describe a number of hands of persons who have found the work in which they could be satisfied. The first is the hand of a successful business man. He has a strong thumb, well balanced, with the will phalanx and the reasoning phalanx of about the same length. He is not unduly obstinate nor is he weak-willed and easily swayed by others. His line of head is straight and firm. That line does not show excess imagination, but rather a utilitarian point of view. His palm is flat and not overly wide, a shape which goes with well-defined interests and concentration on those interests. His heavy Mercury finger with its spatulate tip points to shrewdness and energy in business dealings.

The hand of a popular and versatile actor showed these characteristics: conic, tapered shape, indicating artistic sensitivity; long fingers, wide apart and flexible, showing concern with detail, a broad mind and adaptability; a supple thumb, turned back, indicating good reasoning power and generous exuberance; a long, deeply marked line of head sloping down to the mount of Luna, indicating a vivid and creative imagination.

The hand of a friend of mine, a prominent engineer, is squarely built and practical in shape, giving him order, precision, great determination and perseverance. His line of head is straight, starting some distance above the line of life. Both the Apollo finger and the mount of Mercury are prominent, giving him a sort of instinctive business sense and a practical, scientific mind. It is true that he lacks originality and versatility, but through persistence and good judgment, aided to a considerable extent by sheer good luck, as his strong line of Apollo indicated, he has become remarkably successful.

Another friend of mine, an inventor, also shows a scientific mind, but his other qualities are far different from those of the practical engineer of whom I just spoke. His hand is spatulate, broad, with fairly long, well-developed, widely separated fingers. His outstanding traits are quick decision and action, unconventionality, clear reasoning power, a gift for taking care of detail. His strong line of head, curving slightly upward towards Mercury at its end, gives him an analytical mind and the ability to concentrate.

My barber has a line of head joined to his line of life for a short distance with a slight slope at its end. His fingers are fairly long and tapering. He is an inoffensive, shy man, sympathetic in manner and possessing a strong sense of responsibility.

Of course, it would be impossible for me to give an example of a hand for each profession or trade, much less exhaust all the possibilities for each. Few of us realize how many different vocations there are. That reason, among others, accounts for so many misfits. We choose our life's work out of necessity, taking the first thing which is offered; or in a spirit of emulation, trying what someone we admire has succeeded in; or out of friendship, taking a trade which our best friend has chosen; or out of obedience, letting our parents decide for us. Most of us consider only two or three alternatives before we find ourselves somehow headed in a given direction. I shall make no attempt to list the many thousands of occupations. Below is a partial list of occupations beginning with a, b and c. Such lists can be made for every letter in the alphabet.

author	auctioneer
architect	assayer
artist	automobile mechanic
actor	agent
attorney	aviator
art teacher	accountant

acoustic engineer
adding machine operator
adjuster
advertising counsellor
advertising copywriter
aircraft engineer
animal dealer
animal trainer
antique dealer   ·
appraiser
art needleworker
automobile dealer

banker
baker
broker
beauty specialist
boxmaker
bacteriologist
bagmaker
barber
beverage manufacturer
binder
boilermaker
bondsman
bricklayer
bridgebuilder
broadcaster
broker

buyer

chemist
cartoonist
confectioner
contractor
clock and watchmaker
credit investigator
comptometer operator
civil engineer
clerk
cabinet maker
camera maker
canvasser
carpenter
carpet cleaner
carpet designer
cement contractor
check-room girl
chimney sweep
cigarmaker
chiropractor
chiropodist
claim adjuster
collector
commercial agent
cosmetician
costumer
counterman

Look over this list. Besides these, there are hundreds of other occupations, not even touched on here, others like subdivisions of the ones I have mentioned. Consider yourself in relation to all the vocations you can think of and then study yourself objectively, using the hand as one of your guides, to decide whether you are well fitted for the four or five different callings which seem most to interest you.

In the following pages you will find the hands and analyses of ten world famous personages outstanding in different lines of endeavor. Observe the various signs and lines in their hands that indicate their fame and success.

THE HAND OF FRANKLIN DELANO ROOSEVELT is almost pure spatulate—a most unusual thing in this world of mixed and contradictory personalities. This, of course, shows a person of great independence who necessarily expresses himself in action. As you know, advanced and liberal views go with a spatulate hand, and President Roosevelt is now known throughout the world as an exponent of progress.

As to the fingers, they are quite short and heavy, showing a very broad planning ability, a mind which conceives great projects. Apollo and Mercury are both strong, which tells us that the president is social-minded, that he is of sanguinary temperament and that he is both a gifted orator and though economic royalists might disagree, an excellent business man. The Saturn finger is unusually short. There is nothing of the recluse or introvert in Mr. Roosevelt. And, compared to the Apollo finger, the index finger is also short. I would say that personal ambition is decidedly not one of the president's strong traits. His qualities of leadership are, however, displayed by a heavy mount of Jupiter.

The very free-set, heavy thumb immediately strikes your eye when you study the president's handprint. This shows great generosity, independence and will. His broad, open-minded approach to problems is also borne out by the line of life which curves far out into his hand. At the same time, the line of life is both deep and

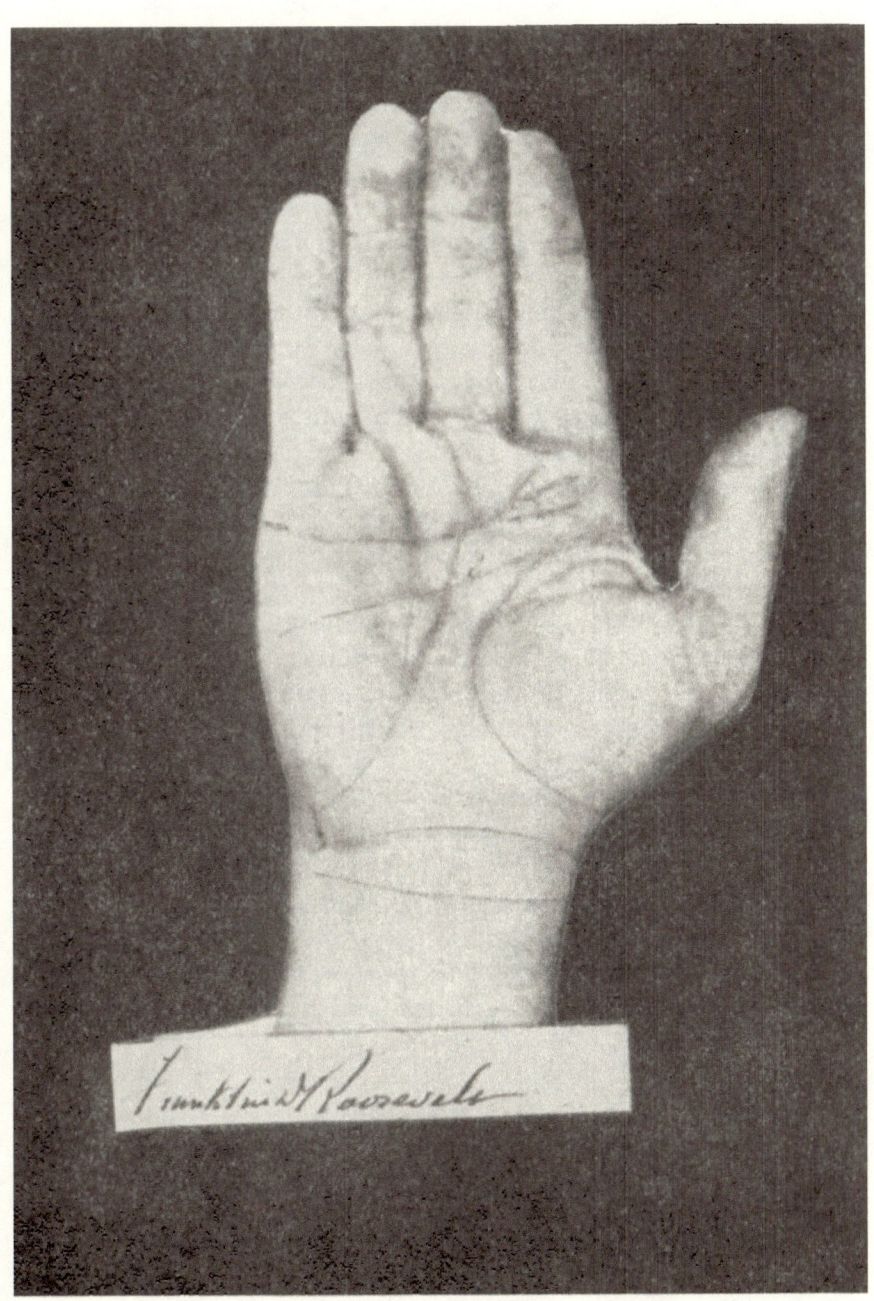

long and is bolstered by the sister line of vitality, indicating remarkable physical endurance.

The line of head, which is unusually long, runs straight across the hand, a sign of excellent, balanced intellect, the ability to think clearly, forcefully and independently. He has an intuitive grasp of things and an immediate understanding of people. He is by no means stubborn. On the contrary, he is very ready to seek and take advance, but he must be convinced that counsel is sound before he will follow it.

The president's line of destiny is a most fortunate one for anyone in a public career. Starting on the mount of Luna, it shows creative force and the helpful influence of others—friends and relatives—in furthering his advancement. The termination of his line of destiny, which joins the line of heart, points to an exceedingly happy marriage, also influential in bringing success. But the line of Apollo, beginning as it does on the line of destiny, says that Mr. Roosevelt himself supplemented the aid from others by his own efforts and is himself greatly responsible for the high place he holds.

Loyalty and idealism characterize Franklin Roosevelt's affections. Notice also the three lines, in trident formation, found at the beginning of Roosevelt's line of heart under the finger of Jupiter. These are the lines of courage, a courage which grows as the obstacles in his way become more difficult.

From the study of his hand I become more and more convinced of the greatness of this man and of the place he will occupy in history. That was my conviction as far back as 1930, when I first studied his hand—that he can truly be counted as one of America's great men and that his name will go down with those of Washington, Jefferson and Lincoln as one who saw his country through a most difficult period and successfully championed its democratic principles.

THE MAN WHO WAS KING does not have a forceful hand. It is of the conic type which goes with a sensitive, company-loving, easily influenced and easily bored nature. The present Duke of

Windsor's hand is rather flat, the mount of Luna being particularly recessive.

The lines are delicate, and there are many fine lines scattered over his palm. This shows a nervous, worrying disposition. The line of life is particularly weak near its beginning, indicating poor health in childhood. There is, in fact, a definite break very close to the point at which the lines of life and head separate, sign of danger when the duke was a boy.

Sensitiveness and lack of self-reliance are shown by the line of head which starts on the line of life and descends to mount Luna. This termination, in conjunction with a poorly developed mount of Luna, indicates moodiness rather than imagination. The many lines descending from the line of head second this indication. So does the cross under the finger of Saturn.

Notice that the thumb is of average length, perhaps a little short, and that its will phalanx bends pliantly out and away from the hand. A person with this type of thumb is easily swayed and influenced by others.

One of the most interesting things about the hand of the Duke of Windsor is that the line of destiny is stopped by the line of heart— interference of the heart with his career. The line of heart is considerably chained and dotted, much more so up to the point where it meets the line of destiny than thereafter. Such a chained line of heart, and the fickleness which usually goes with it, is hardly indicative of an adult's well-controlled emotions. I would say that the Duke of Windsor's hand is that of a man who never grew up. He belongs to the "lost generation," whose formative years were lived in the hell of Europe's great war. That generation faced death daily and for relaxation turned to irresponsible extravagances and pleasures. Denied the right to plan their lives and take responsibilities seriously, they refused to become adult. So with Edward Windsor. The war stunted his growth as a person. He rebelled against submerging himself in the pomp and display of his office. He insisted on his right as an individual to duck responsibility for marriage and personal happiness.

There are two short lines of "marriage" or sex influence on the side of his hand, so that I should say that there are or have been or are to be two women in his life.

H.R.H. EDWARD Duke Of Windsor
Enzesfeld, Austria

The lines of restlessness or "travel" are very numerous on the lower edge of his hand.

But, if you look closely, you will see many squares in this hand—signs of preservation which modify many of the negative qualities. From these and the triangle at the base of the line of life, I would judge that Edward, Duke of Windsor, may still play an important part in world affairs if he asserts his own personality and allows himself to grow up.

THE HAND OF ADOLF HITLER is in many respects a fateful hand. It is of the elementary conic or artistic type with tapering fingers and thick, fleshy bases, denoting emotionalism, selfishness, passion. The two outstanding mounts are found under the fingers of Jupiter and Saturn. The first indicates boundless ambition, a domineering, bullying disposition demanding blind submission from everyone. The second shows moodiness, wide swings from one emotional extreme to another, suicidal morbidity at one moment, then fanatic self-adulation, meglomania.

Hitler's line of life terminates in a cross, which may be the sign of a violent end. The line of head terminates in an island which indicates some kind of weakness—functional or organic—of the brain. The line of heart, which is short, islanded and broken, shows frustration, bitterness and cruelty. The broken, distorted girdle of Venus above the line of heart accentuates the destructiveness and unnaturalness of this hand.

Most remarkable of all is the line of destiny whose origin is marked by a cross, its termination by a star under the middle finger. This line marks the destiny of a man whose fate is out of his control. He is marked out for an awful, tragic role. The destiny line, you will note, stretches unbroken and bare from its tragic beginning to its violent end.

I do not want to make too detailed an analysis of this man Hitler's hand because I fear that others, finding signs similar to one or

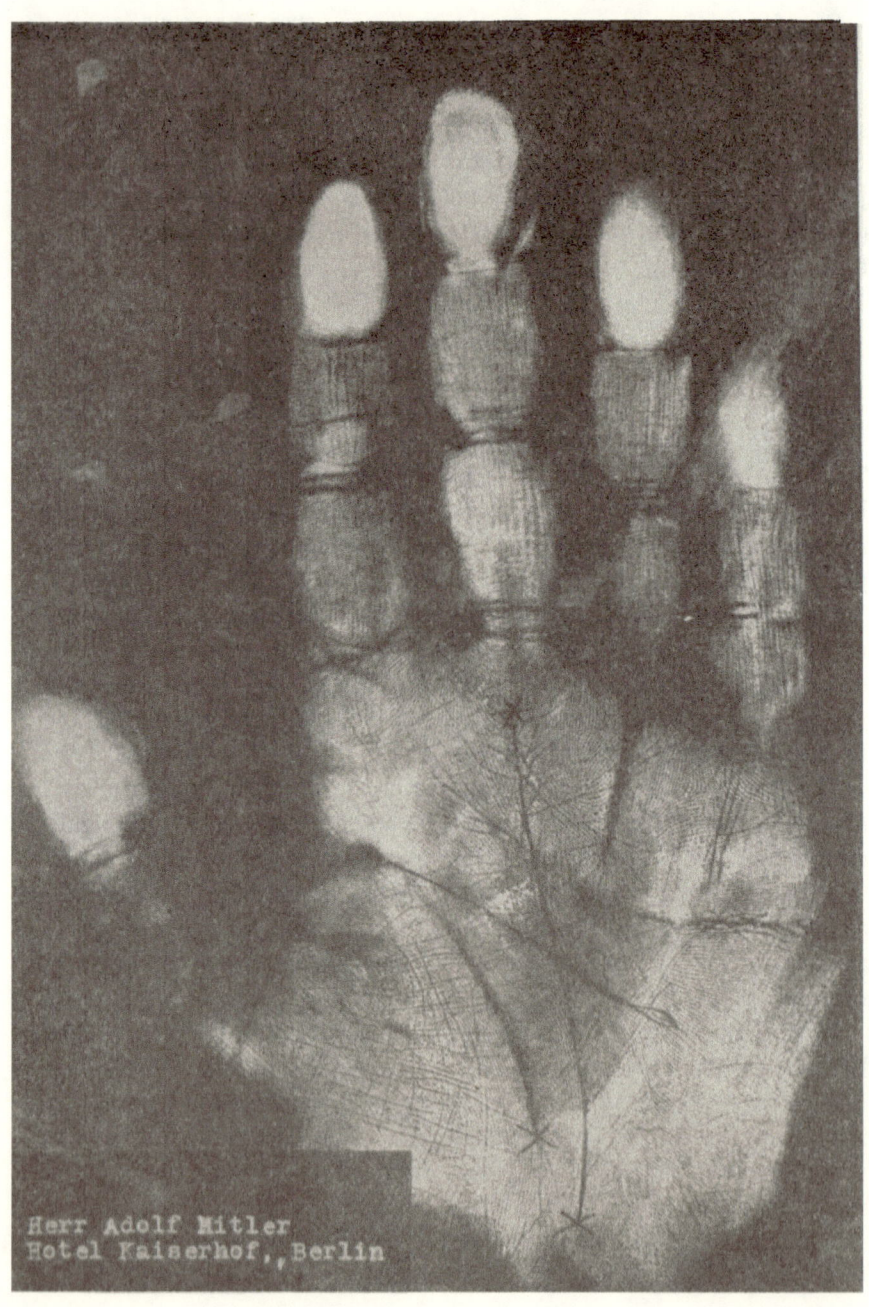

Herr Adolf Mitler
Hotel Kaiserhof, Berlin

two of Hitler's in their own hands may assign to themselves the qualities which make Hitler what he is. For this reason, I wish again to emphasize that no single sign or set of signs can be read apart from the indications of the hand as a whole. It is only from the study of the totality of a hand that an accurate analysis can be made.

BENITO MUSSOLINI'S HAND combines the spatulate and the conic shapes. He has the vanity of the conic-handed and the energy and strength of the spatulate with which to satisfy his vanity. The base phalanxes of the spatulate fingers are thick and fleshy, the fingertips broad and flat. His hands speak of action, movement, boundless energy and restlessness. But even more than that, they tell of determination at the cost of humanity, of strength which is brutality.

The line of Apollo shows three distinct phases. Its start, on the line of life, points out the self-made man. There is a sharp change of direction covering the years from the age of about twenty-five to forty. Then comes another new direction, almost a new line, growing out of the old. This seems to apply to the period from the age of forty to the late fifties. After that there is no more. This robust son of a blacksmith was about forty when his blackshirts marched on Rome and he became premier. That happened some sixteen years ago.

The line of destiny, which is exceedingly strong at the period between the ages of forty and the late fifties, also ends abruptly at about the same time as the line of Apollo. Mussolini's is an historic destiny, achieved by blood and force and, I am convinced, short-lived in its duration.

The most interesting things about the lines of life and head are the breaks, invariably healed by squares. These show escapes from dangers, narrow escapes from violence. But if you look closely you will see a final break, especially apparent in the line of head, which is not fenced in by a protecting square. Once—and that is all that

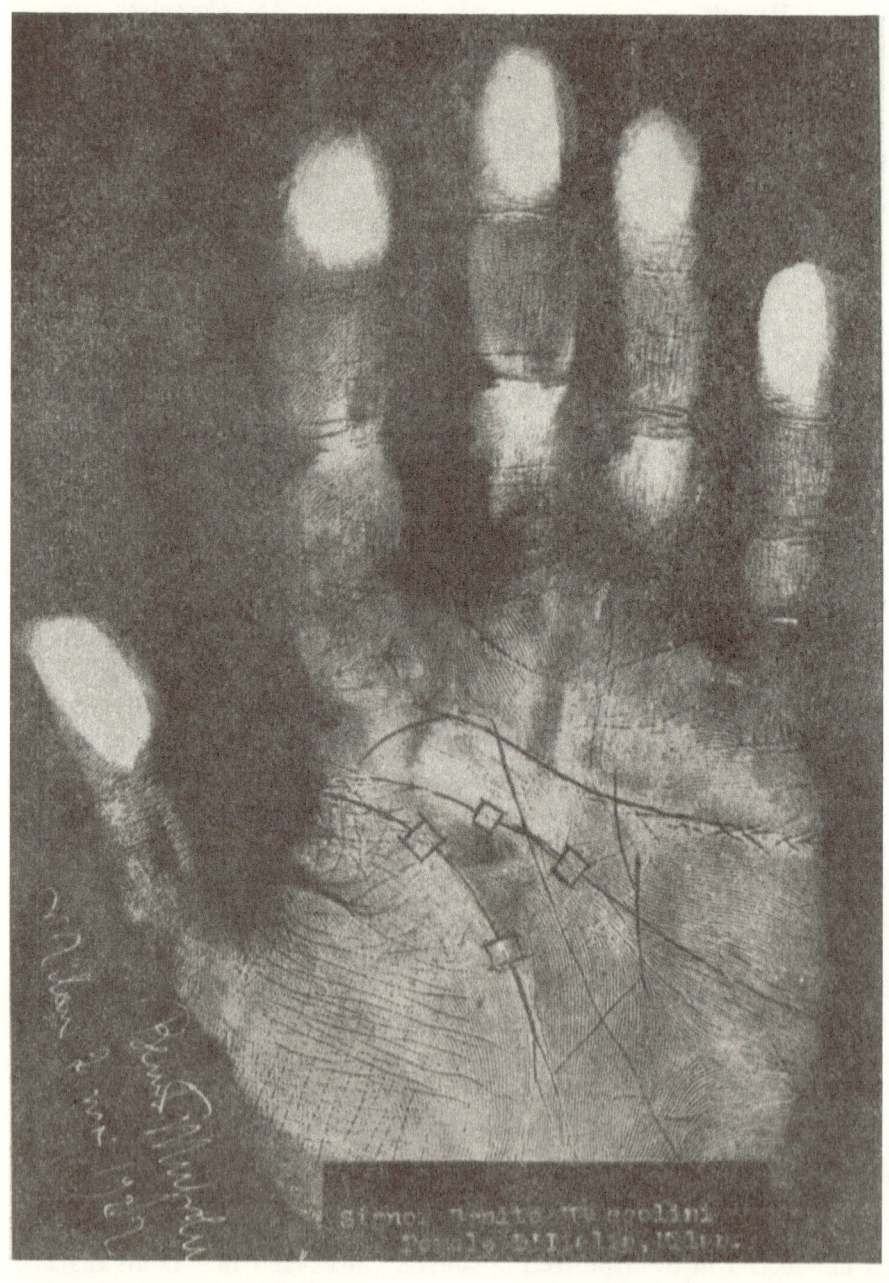

any man is allowed—there is only the violence and no sign of escape from it.

A few other details are of interest. The strong downward curving fork at the beginning of the heart line shows a violent temper. The star at the base of the first finger shows qualities of leadership, and the use of force in imposing that leadership. The clearly marked, almost unbroken girdle of Venus and the predominant mount, Venus at the base of the thumb, indicate an oversexed, violent person. Mussolini's hand is clearly a hand of destiny, but hardly of an altogether happy destiny.

IN PARIS IN 1929, I interviewed most of the French leading personalities, statesmen, scientists, politicians, etc. Among them was the then president of the French Senate, M. Paul Doumer. He had a very unusual hand, in some respects, a very tragic hand. The lines, especially the break in the heartline, indicated a strange fatality. At the time, he was already past the age of 70 and one of the most beloved characters in France. He had given the lives of four sons to France during the World War. He was known as a capable administrator. He was personally most charming.

His hand indicated that he would reach the highest honors within the reach of a Frenchman—and that his subsequent end would be tragic.

I was rather startled by that hand. M. Doumer noticed my puzzled expression. Jokingly, he told me that I could tell him anything I saw, for he had been told by Mme. Thebes, a famous hand analyst of Paris, many years ago, that he would have a violent end. He shrugged his shoulders and laughed as much as to say, "What terrors can death hold for a man who has reached three score years and ten and lived through everything I have seen?" Despite his philosophic attitude, I saw no need to be brutally direct and told him that all the lines in his hand indicated some terrific shock but that I really did not know what to say about it. We had a most interesting conversation, and then we parted.

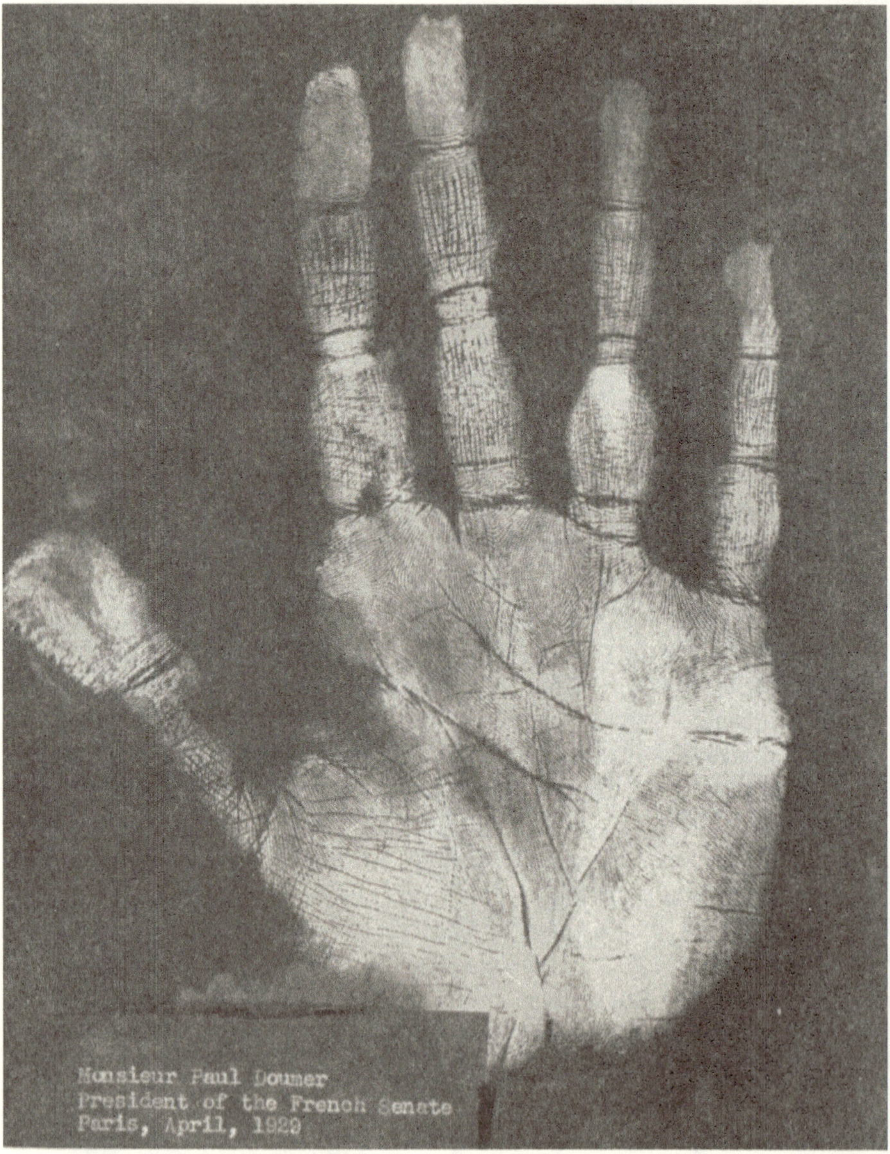

Monsieur Paul Doumer
President of the French Senate
Paris, April, 1929

Two years later, while writing *Hands of Destiny*, a feature of mine syndicated by World Feature Service and the United Features Syndicate, in which I gave analyses of famous hands, I came across the impression of M. Doumer's hand. He had by then been elected president of France, thus fulfilling one of the promises of his hand. In starting my analysis, I intimated what the break in the heartline meant. The feature went to more than one hundred newspapers carrying it.

A few weeks later, Paul Doumer was assassinated by a madman. Naturally, my seemingly prophetic story then caused quite a sensation among the various newspaper editors.

One thing I should like to stress—that I do not go in for predictions and certainly do not go around foretelling violent death or assassination; but in this case, if the lines of the hand were of any significance, they certainly indicated a very tragic and sudden end. As the reader can see by the breaks in all the lines, especially noticeable in the lines of heart and of life, all occurring at about the same time, some sort of fatality was indicated for that time.

A few other indications in this remarkable hand are noteworthy. The hand was square in general shape, the fingers somewhat pointed, giving him extreme practicality and keen, intuitive insight. The triangle at the base of the third finger, showing administrative ability is an interesting mark. Mount Venus, at the base of the thumb, was the most prominent eminence of this hand, showing a person of great physical vigor. Altogether, these qualities help explain the peasant boy who became president of France and lost his life at the hands of a maniac.

KATHARINE CORNELL'S is one of the most eloquent hands I have ever seen. In type, it most closely resembles the conic and knotty. From this you can build a personality which, while extremely sensitive to the moods and feelings of others, yet possesses a profound and independent mental life of its own. There is great spiritual strength in this hand.

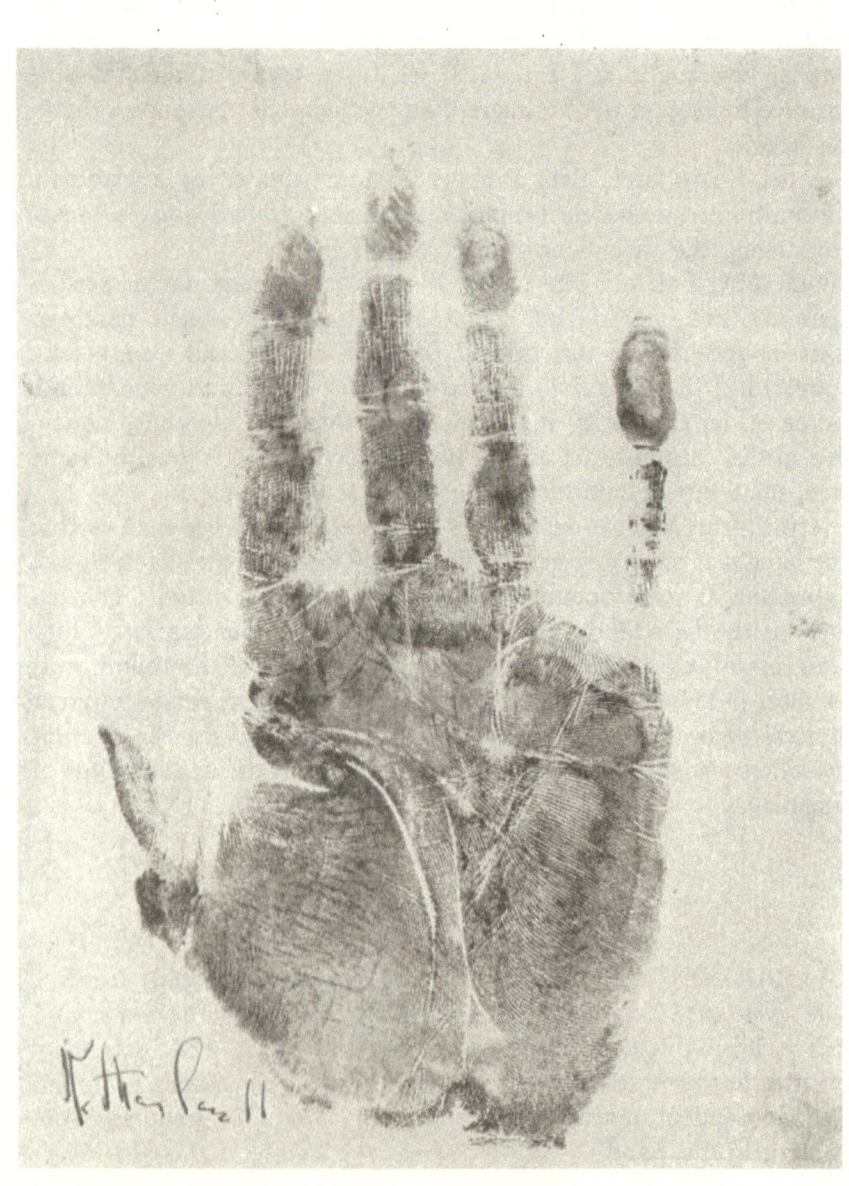

The lines of the hand are clear and deep. The line of life, which has great strength after it passes the early years, indicates a robust physical constitution and unusual personal magnetism. The line of heart, which goes up between the bases of the first and second fingers, gives Miss Cornell deep, unsentimental, sensitive feeling. In its independence from the line of head, this line of heart indicates that she has great emotional stability. Her balance allows neither emotional extravagances nor temperamental outbursts.

The line of head is a fitting one for an actress. Its early junction with the line of life shows sensitivity. The slight slope towards the mount of imagination adds that quality, so necessary for a career on the stage.

The line of destiny, which begins with one branch from the mount of imagination, is also an excellent indication for an actress. It indicates not only the part imaginative thinking and feeling play in her career but also the helpful influence of others in building that career —the aid of appreciative audiences, of a producer husband whose interests are so closely bound with hers.

The most unusual mark in Miss Cornell's hand is the semicircle ringing the base of her first finger—the ring of Solomon. This gives her intuitive understanding of dramatic values and emotional grasp. Strangely enough, this mark is present in the hand of Greta Garbo and was to be seen under Sarah Bernhardt's first finger. Whenever an actress is able to project to her audience an inner beauty and spirituality, I look for this mark.

Another interesting sign in Miss Cornell's hand is the cross at the base of her third finger which indicates a very keen sense of observation. From this I would judge that her impersonations are based not only on intuitive understanding, but also on study of reality. The ability to represent what she feels and sees is aided by a flowing ease of expression, indicated by her long finger of Mercury.

FANNIE HURST'S HAND is knotty and conic in its predominant characteristics. This combination gives her both the independence of thought and the sensitive understanding of people which her writings show. The palm of the hand, you will notice, is covered with a fine network of delicate lines, showing her intensity, partly nervous, and her openness to impressions from things and conditions around her. Her lined hand is also an indication of early struggles and uncertainty.

The first finger, though smaller than the second, is slightly larger than the third. This indicates strong ambition. But the square under the first finger, while it does not lessen the ambition, counteracts whatever bitterness there might be from failure to achieve success in all its desired aspects. The long finger of Mercury is the outward symbol of Miss Hurst's ease of expression.

Miss Hurst's line of life, circling the heel of the thumb, is delicate, though very clear and without breaks, indicating strong resistance and vitality. The line of head, which begins on the line of life, shows sensitiveness early in life and lack of self-confidence. The clear and independent path taken by the line of head later on indicates her growing independence and self-reliance. Notice that the headline splits at its termination, sending one branch towards the mount of imagination, the other to the negative mount of Mars, portraying her qualities of deepseeing imagination and moral courage.

Miss Hurst's line of heart is slightly chained, though the quality of the line is forceful. I should say that Miss Hurst is not altogether consistent in her emotions, though her feelings are intense. The termination of the line of heart at the base of the first finger indicates a strong sense of social responsibility.

A number of special signs have unusual significance in Miss Hurst's hand. The line of intuition is very well defined, and there is a cross, usually associated with keen observation, under the third finger. Thus, Miss Hurst has at her command three qualities invaluable to a writer: fluency, observation—a basis for realism, and intuitive understanding. The triangle between the line of destiny and the line of intuition shows Miss Hurst's ability to apply her understanding in telling fashion.

Miss Hurst's thumb is a very strong one. The joint is knotty, showing a somewhat philosophic and abstract trend to her reasoning. The will phalanx is well developed. The setting is low and free, sign of a generous, uninhibited nature.

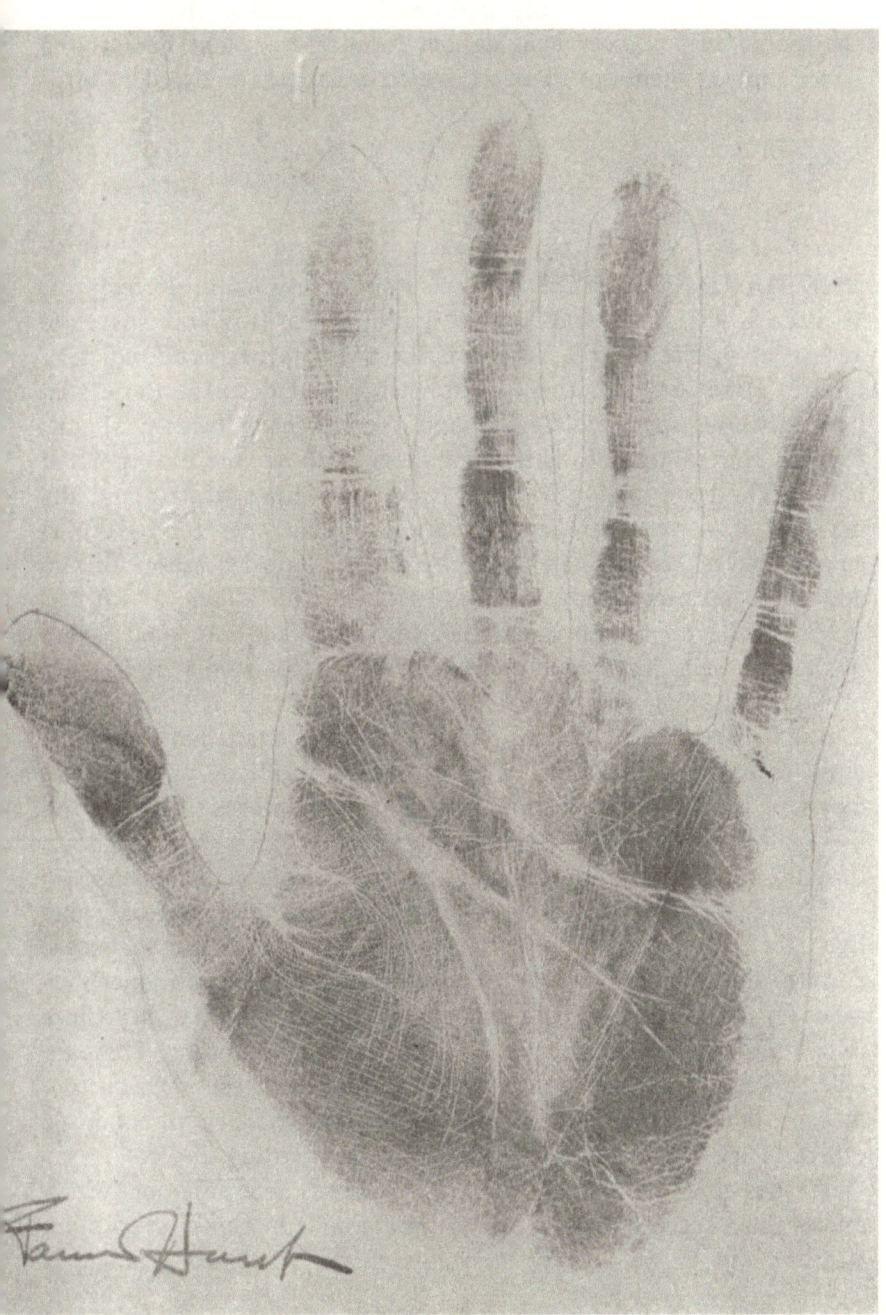

Two mounts are especially well developed in Miss Hurst's hand: the mount of Luna, or imagination, forming the outer heel of the hand; and the mount of Mercury, which designates an excellent business sense.

THE HAND POSSESSED by Secretary of Agriculture Henry A. Wallace is a most unusual combination of types. It is both spatulate and pointed, disclosing a most complex and somewhat contradictory nature. Here are both the furious energy and drive of those who have spready, spatulate hands; and the insight, intuition, almost, psychic powers and idealistic dreaminess of those who have pointed hands. The combination of these two types—the spatulate and the psychic—is a very rare and a very beautiful one. Its beauty is emphasized in Mr. Wallace's hand by almost perfect balance. Fingers and palm are exceedingly well proportioned.

Mr. Wallace's thumb is flexible, with both the first and second phalanxes well developed, revealing fairly strong will power and brilliant reasoning ability.

But it is really in the lines of Mr. Wallace's hand that I find the most revealing indications of his complex, brilliant and unusual makeup. His lifeline is very long and clear, reinforced by a second line—the line of vitality—inside the line of life. This should indicate long life, almost boundless energy, action and accomplishment.

When you look for the head- and heartlines, you find only one line—the two joined into one. This in itself is a very unusual feature—in any hand. In Mr. Wallace's hand it denotes tremendous intensity of purpose. Those who have their head- and heartlines joined into one possess, above all, great capacity for work. They are able to keep their own counsel. They are at their best when on top, in executive positions, not hampered by the rule and direction of others. They shine by their daring ideas and strong ideals.

At the same time, they have a persistent determination which makes them succeed against overwhelming odds in almost everything they set out to do. I have seen this single, combined heart- and

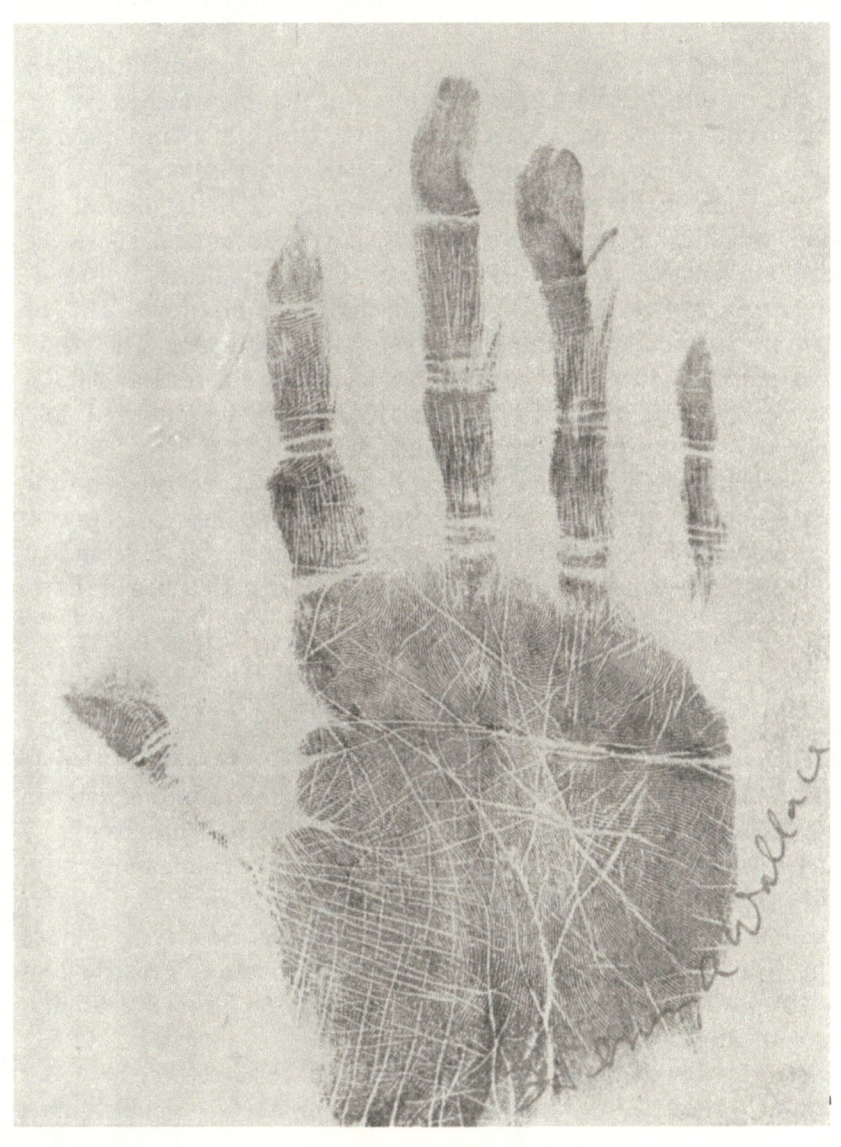

headline in hands of outstanding leaders—generals, captains of industry, and the like—and, in whatever endeavor they find themselves, they always leave an indelible mark of their personality and efforts.

That Mr. Wallace's hand is a hand of great potentialities and brilliant future success is seen first of all in the line which starts off from his line of life and runs strongly to the base of his third finger—a line of brilliancy and a sure sign of success and fame.

There are many squares, found especially in the center of his hand, which are marks of preservation. The triangle seen above the headline, between the second and third fingers, indicates outstanding administrative ability. The square under the first finger tells us that he will not let his ambitions run away with him. The many lines found at the outer edge of his hand show a restless nature, not satisfied with things as they are if they can be improved, and also point to the probability of much travel.

In summing up, I want to say that, basing my conclusions on the totality of the shape and on the formation of the lines in Henry A. Wallace's hand, I would not be surprised to see his outstanding abilities rewarded with the highest honors this nation has to offer.

THE HAND WHICH GOES WITH THE VOICE that tells movie and radio audiences about all the big events in the sports world is one of the luckiest I have ever seen. Not that luck is all there is to be seen in Lowell Thomas' hand. In type, it is a combination, and a rather unusual one, of the spatulate and knotty shapes. If you refer back to the section in which hand types are discussed, you will see why this combination is out of the ordinary. It means a marriage of action with thought—not just business and administrative ability, but profound, original thinking.

Furthermore, Lowell Thomas' line of head tells me that he is not just a theoretician so far as sports are concerned. The double curve, first down, then up, to be found at the end of his line of head gives him that perfect coordination of mind and muscle which is necessary

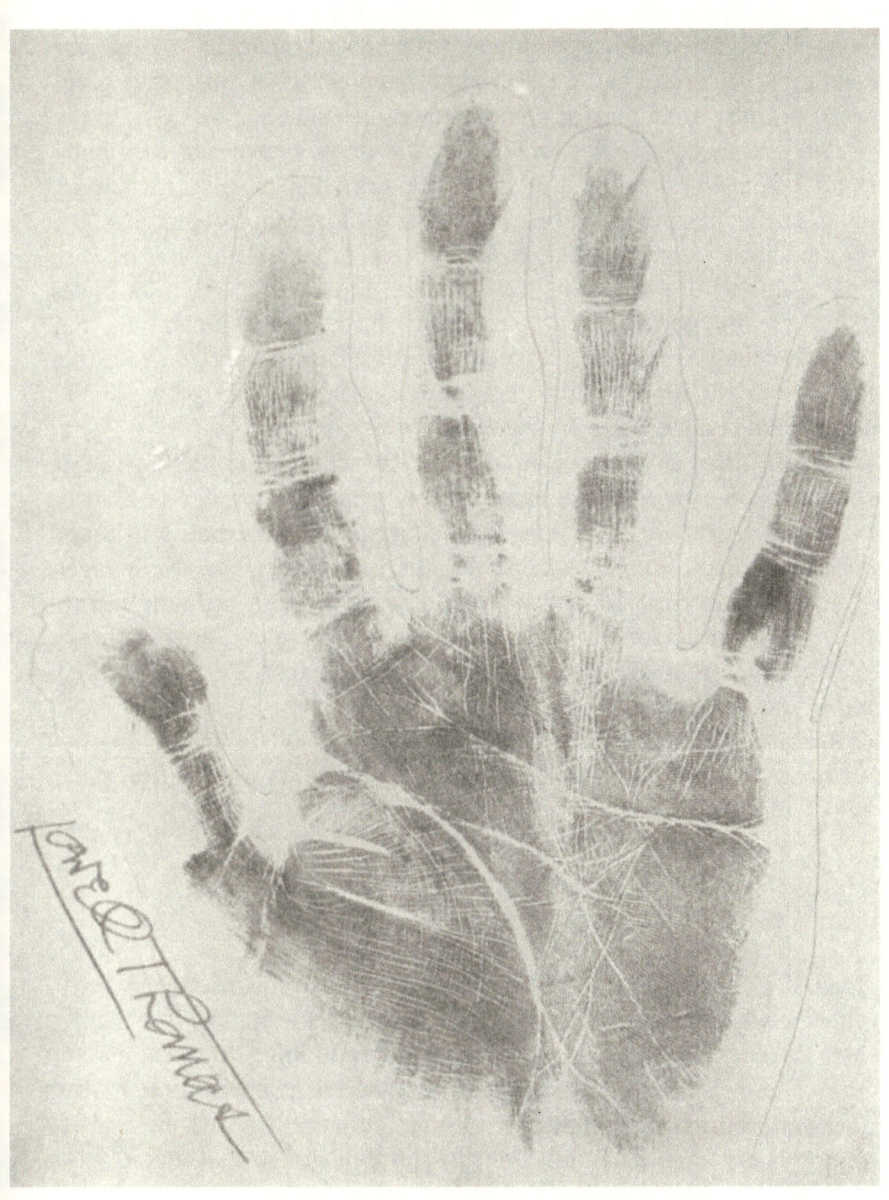

to the champion athlete. The quality of the line of head is excellent, clear, deep and unbroken.

The lifeline in Lowell Thomas' hand is one of his strongest. But notice the island near its beginning. From this I judge that, like other men of action, Thomas will encounter serious danger during the course of his life. The square right in the center of his hand gives every promise that he will come through all right.

The heartline, with its fork under the index finger and the many small leader-lines going into it, is the heartline of a spirited man, loyal in friendship and well endowed with physical courage. The thumb shows strong temper, easily aroused but quick to subside.

The line of destiny, starting from the mount of imagination, goes up to a point between the second and third fingers, indicating that Mr. Thomas' fate is not altogether under his own control. Yet, fate has been very kind to him. His career has been aided by friends, and circumstances have furthered his success.

Lowell Thomas' line of Apollo, which starts from the fortunate square in the center of his hand and runs up in a number of parallel branches to the base of his third finger, indicates both luck and versatility. And notice the star on this line, under the third finger. A star in this position, I have found to be a most brilliant sign of fame, honors and fortune. The triangle at the base of Thomas' line of life indicates that he may at some future date test this good luck of his in some public capacity.

And, last, look at the long, independent little finger in Mr. Thomas' hand. This goes with the fluent ease of expression for which Mr. Thomas is famous.

WALT DISNEY'S HAND is the fortunate combination of knotty-philosophic and spatulate. This is indeed a lucky duality, for it gives Mr. Disney the capacity for independent thinking plus the energy and courage for action. Too many thinkers live in a world of abstract ideas and do not contribute directly to the world we live in; and too many of our men of action are incapable of arriving at sound bases

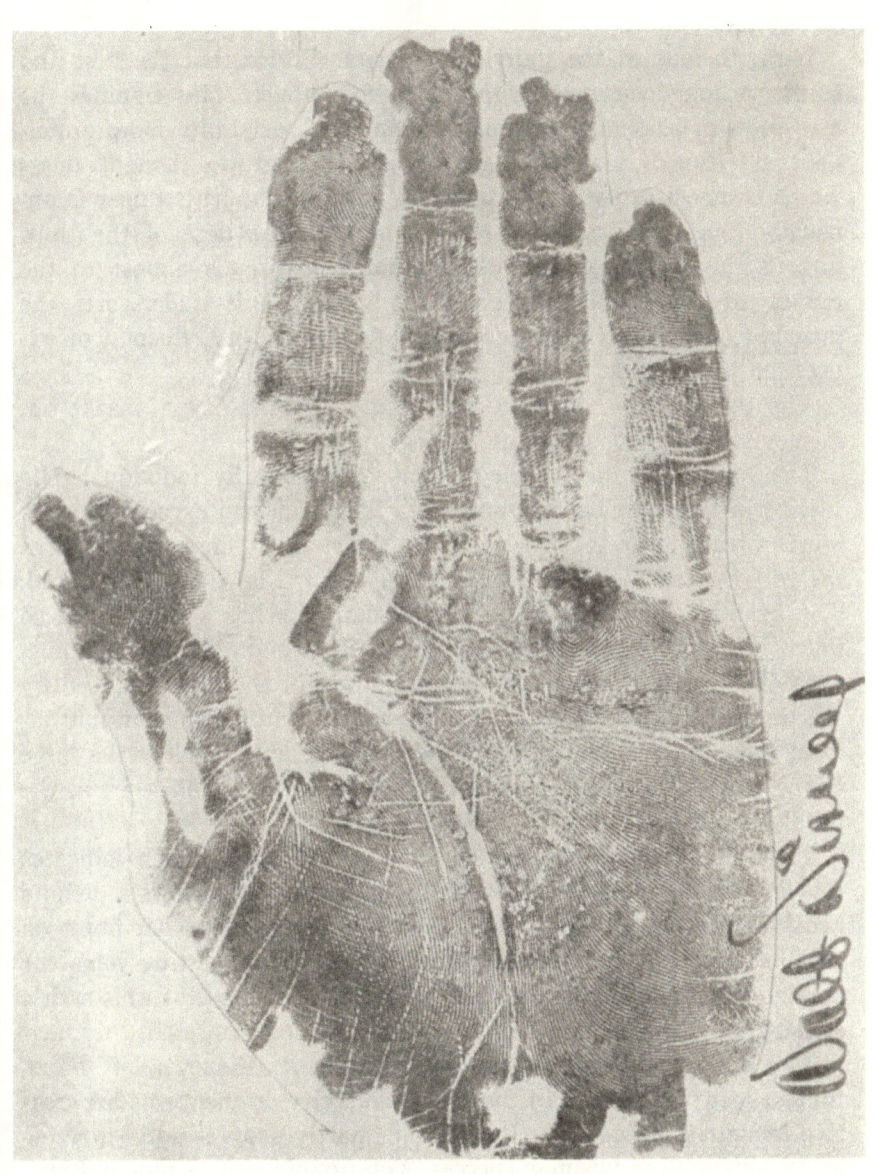

for their activities. From the creator of the world's most popular comedians, Mickey Mouse and his troupe, we can expect both originality and action.

Now, to look at the individual fingers. Notice that the first and third are long compared with the middle finger. This signifies the attributes of leadership, dramatic talent and sociability more prominent in Disney's makeup than the serious, ingrown thoughtfulness which is associated with the finger of Saturn. The little finger is unusually long. Ordinarily, it reaches only to the base of the third finger's first phalanx. In Disney's hand it extends almost to the middle of the Apollo finger's first phalanx. This underscores the prominence of Mercurial qualities: business ability, fluency of expression and humor.

The thumb, which is of a pronounced spatulate type, marks out Disney's courageous and enterprising nature.

The lines of Walter Disney's hand are markedly individual. His lifeline in the right hand is unusually long and firm except for some minor breaks near the beginning. It shows great improvement over the very broken lifeline in his left hand, which I have not reproduced. The headline, strangely enough in a man who has accomplished so much in public ways, is closely tied to the lifeline at its beginning, even showing portions which penetrate within the area enclosed by the line of life. This shows a supersensitive nature which would almost have made a hermit of Disney were it not offset by the large triangle of humor seen connecting the lines of head and heart at the base of the second finger.

The line of heart is set pretty low in the hand, which indicates that Mr. Disney is quite emotional. The destiny line shows a definite break at the line of head and a new beginning at another point on the line of head. This second part of the line of destiny joins the triangle of humor and shows how Disney found himself in his satiric artistry, and how he won success through it.

The girdle of Venus is quite noticeable in Disney's left hand, though less pronounced in the right. This gives evidence of his creative imagination, which he has perhaps partly suppressed in arriving at an outstanding business success. The prominence of mount Luna, along the outer edge of the hand, however, also attests to an active imagination which finds expression in the thousand and one humorous details in his cartoon-comedies.

But even more important than the mount of Luna in Disney's hand is the mount of Apollo, whose fullness is directly under the Apollo finger. This mount is usually to be found between the base of the second and third fingers. When it occurs directly under the third finger it is an exceedingly fortunate indication. In Disney's hand it probably more than makes up for the absence of the Apollo line.

There are many lines of restlessness along the outer edge of Disney's hand, and he will probably travel about, perhaps go in for exploration or flying fairly late in life. But whatever he does, the saving grace of humor, so prominently designated by the triangle of which I have already spoken, will temper his actions and his thoughts.

PART SIX

How to Make Imprints and Analyze Your Hand

IN studying your hand, be sure to examine every portion of it, but do not let the details confuse you. First, form an estimate of the hand as a whole, then relate the variations of your lines, fingers, mounts and markings to that whole.

The back of the hand makes a good starting point, for it will tell the general type of your hand. Note the length and heaviness of the fingers in proportion to the palm and in relation to each other. Examine the joints. Are they prominent, or are the fingers smooth? What is the quality of your skin? Coarse or fine? But do not let artificial coarsening of the skin from exposure to cold, wind or materials used in your work confuse you. Look carefully at the nails.

Now feel the hand and the fingers. Are they stiff and uncompromising or supple? Note whether the fingers bend back easily at all the points or more at one than at another. Are the fingers wide apart or close together? Are they straight or crooked? Do some lean or bend towards others?

Now, turn the hand and look at the palm. What is the first impression you get of it? Is it long and narrow or wide? Is it square, oval, tapering or spready in shape? Notice its color. Look at it in relief. Are the mounts prominent or is your palm flat in appearance? Is the flesh firm and elastic or flabby?

Look again at the fingers from the palmar side, repeating all the observations you made of them from the back. Pay special attention to the thumb. Is it set low? Is it set free or close to the hand? Is it long or short, and which is its longest and heaviest phalanx?

Now turn to the lines. First, before examining them individually, form a general impression of their quality and number. Is your palm marked with many fine lines or are there few? Are most of them clear and firm or are they broken up, broad and shallow, feathered, islanded or interrupted by dots? Study the lines in relation to each other. Which are longest and strongest? What is the general pattern formed by the principal lines of your hand?

Do this with both your hands, comparing the two carefully. The left hand shows inherited tendencies. On it you will see the characteristics and tendencies transmitted to you by your parents. From the right hand, you can judge the variations you have composed on the main motifs shown in your left. You will be able to tell whether or not you have made the most of your potentialities, whether you have fulfilled the promise of your left hand. If you are left-handed, of course reverse the significance of the two hands, for the left will then be the operative one.

All these preliminary observations you can make from the hand itself. There is, however, only one accurate way of carefully analyzing the hand. That is from a clear imprint. A good impression will bring out the major lines of the hand, pointing up their differences in quality. Moreover, a good print gives you a permanent record which you can compare with later prints as time goes on. A series of impressions of the same hand taken at regular intervals over a number of years is a much more telling record of your development than is a photograph album. The lines of the hand change as you change.

For that reason, I urge everyone to keep such a record of himself. It not only makes an interesting memento, but it actually gives you a diagnosis of your physical and mental development. From careful comparison of the prints, you should be able to reorientate yourself if you have strayed off the path of constructive development, for you will clearly see the minute changes in yourself which are making you into a different person.

You may want to send an impression to me for analysis. Your own study of the hand will tell you much. What I can give you in addition is the knowledge gained through study of thousands of impressions of prominent persons all over the world. Because the publishers foresaw that you might wish to have me examine your handprint, they have made arrangements by which I can give you a general analysis, based on the general type of your hand and the outstanding trends revealed in its lines.

And now for the method of making hand impressions. I have included in this book eight sheets of paper sensitized by a process which I invented for the purpose. On this paper, you can make an impression of your hand without in any way staining or soiling it. The directions are simple. For best results, prepare a solution of soda —one teaspoonful of bicarbonate or the plain washing or baking variety of soda—in a tumblerful of glycerine. The glycerine, which is quite inexpensive and can be bought at any drugstore, makes the clearest impressions. If you do not want to trouble about glycerine, lukewarm, soapy water, in the same proportions, will give an adequate handprint.

After you have dissolved the teaspoonful of soda in the liquid, wet a corner of your handkerchief or some other small piece of cloth and moisten your hand—left or right, whichever is the one you use for writing and other activities. Be sure to avoid excess moisture, as too much liquid will blur the impression.

Place a pad of four thicknesses of turkish towelling under the impression paper. Then put your hand, palm down with the fingers slightly spread, on the sensitized sheet. Press down the hand with an even, light pressure, gently applying extra pressure with the other hand to the fingertips and palm. Be sure that you do not shift your hand while you are making the print.

After you have removed your hand, allow the print to dry for about an hour. When you are quite sure that it is dry, replace your hand in exactly the same position as you had it in when you made the print. Now, with a pencil, carefully trace the outline of your hand as it rests on the paper. When you are finished, you will have a complete print, the impression giving you the lines, markings and eminences of the fingers and the palm within the pencil outline which you have just added.

The first thing to do now is to write your name and the date on the back of the sheet of paper so that you will be able to refer to the impression in the future. Then try to analyze the print or, if you wish, send it to me for an analysis.